A PARENT'S STEP-BY-STEP GUIDE TO

THE

USING GRADES 9–12 TO PREPARE YOUR

LIFE-READY

CHILD FOR COLLEGE, A CAREER, AND

KID

EVERYTHING THAT COMES AFTER

EILEEN RESTREPO, M.ED.

Copyright © 2026 by Eileen Restrepo

All rights reserved. This publication is designed to provide accurate and authoritative information in regard to the subject matter covered. It is provided with the understanding that neither the author nor the publisher is engaged in rendering legal, financial, medical, or other professional services. While the author and publisher have used their best efforts in preparing this book, they make no representations or warranties with respect to the accuracy or completeness of the contents. The advice and strategies contained herein may not be suitable for your specific situation. You should consult a qualified professional where appropriate. Neither the author nor the publisher shall be liable for any losses or damages resulting from the use of this information.

Published independently.

ISBN: 979-8-950531-01-9

Book Cover Design and Interior Formatting by 100Covers

Table of Contents

Introduction

You're Not Behind — You're Right on Time

Nobody gives you a manual for this part of parenting.

You get a baby, and people hand you books about sleep schedules and feeding. You get a toddler, and there are guides for tantrums and potty training. But somewhere between the first day of high school and the college application deadline, most parents are completely on their own. No roadmap. No instructions. Just a teenager who may or may not be talking to you, a pile of confusing information from the internet, and a clock that suddenly feels like it's moving way too fast.

If that sounds familiar, you're in the right place.

The fact that you picked up this book says something real about you. It says you care enough to look for answers when you don't have them. It says you're not willing to just hope things work out. And it says that your kid's future matters to you more than your comfort, more than your pride, and more than the awkwardness of admitting you don't fully understand a system that everyone else seems to navigate just fine. That's not a small thing. Most parents never get this far. They worry, they lose sleep, they argue with their teenager about grades, but they never actually sit down and try to learn what's really going on. You did.

So no, you're not behind. You're right on time.

There's a particular kind of parent who picks up a book like this one. Maybe you grew up in a working class family, never went to a four-year school yourself, and now you're trying to navigate a system that wasn't built for people like you, without a guide, without connections, and without the luxury of expensive private counselors who charge more per hour than you make in a day. Or maybe, like my own parents, you came to this country with almost nothing and built a life through sheer stubbornness and sacrifice. College isn't just a goal. It's the whole point. It's the thing that makes every hard year worth it. Maybe you're the parent who's already done everything right on paper. You hired the tutors, signed up them up for test prep, but you still feel like you missed something and can't figure out what it is. Or maybe you're just a parent who loves their kid and is terrified of getting this wrong.

You are all welcome here.

What if my child doesn't want a four year college?

Just in case you're wondering if this information applies to your child—a child who is currently interested in careers that don't require a four-year degree—this book can help too. What most kids don't understand is that while applying to a two-year program at a community college, trade, or technical college may seem easier, they still need financial aid, and they still are going to need the life skills I've outlined in this book.

As a working adult, you know what has made you successful in your career. Whether you work in a trade or a small office, you need certain skills. Communication, adaptability, teamwork, problem-solving, emotional intelligence, and time management are the skills that help people keep jobs, grow professionally, work well with others, and handle stress and change. These are not just "college skills." They are real-life skills that help young adults succeed no matter what path they choose after high school.

Because every student's path looks different, not every section of this book will apply equally to every family. Feel free to move past the four-year college-specific material if it does not fit your child's goals and focus instead on the sections that feel most useful and relevant for your family.

The fear you're carrying right now is real. The worry that your teen isn't motivated enough, isn't building the right profile, isn't doing what other kids seem to be doing, that fear comes from love. It's not a character flaw.

It's what happens when you care deeply about someone whose future you can't fully control.

But here's what most of the books and articles and YouTube videos won't tell you: that fear, when you don't understand the system, tends to make things worse, not better. It leads to nagging. It leads to fights. It leads to a teenager who shuts down every time you bring up college because they've learned that the conversation always ends the same way.

Understanding the system changes that. When you know what actually matters and why, you stop panicking about the wrong things. You start having different conversations. You start showing up for your kid in ways that actually help instead of ways that just relieve your own anxiety for a few hours.

That shift starts here, with this book, right now.

The next four years of your child's life are not a high-stakes competition where one wrong move ends everything. They're one of the most powerful seasons you'll ever have as a parent. Your teenager is still at home. They still need you, even when they act like they don't. The habits they build right now, the way they handle pressure, the way they talk about themselves, the way they get back up after something doesn't go their way, those things are being shaped in real time. And you have more influence over that than you probably realize. This is what this book is about: using that influence wisely.

What This Book Will Do for You (and Why It's Different)

You've probably seen the advice before. "Start early." "Get involved in extracurriculars." "Make sure your essays are authentic." I admit it. I've used those words too. When speaking with high school students and their parents it's easy for teachers, counselors and specialists to boil down college admissions to these few phrases. But we usually don't have the time to explain what we really mean. There are great school programs out there, like GEAR UP and AVID that try and fill that gap but they can be limited by class size and staffing. And the reality is that you are still the most influential person in your kid's life. I'm sure right now you're thinking: okay but what can I do? What do those words actually mean? What does "start early" look like on a Tuesday night when your kid has homework and you have dinner to make and nobody has time for a strategy session? What activities actually matter? What does "authentic" mean when your teenager doesn't even know who they are yet?

Vague advice doesn't help anyone. This book isn't that.

What you'll get here is a clear, grade-by-grade picture of what matters when You'll understand what colleges are actually looking for now — not ten years ago, not based on rumors from other parents, but based on how modern admissions really works. You'll learn what "holistic review" means in plain terms. You'll find out why a 4.0 GPA or perfect test scores alone don't guarantee anything anymore, and what actually moves the needle when an admissions reader is sitting with your child's file. You'll understand the difference between a student who looks good on paper and a student who has a story worth telling.

You'll also get something that most college prep books skip entirely: a real conversation about money. Scholarships, financial aid, FAFSA, merit money, how to compare award letters without a finance degree. If you've ever looked at a college's sticker price and felt your stomach drop, this book will help you understand that the sticker price is almost never the real price, and that knowing how to read the numbers can change which schools actually make sense for your family.

There's a section in this book about letting go that might be the most important thing you read all year.

Not because letting go is easy. It isn't. But because the research on what makes students succeed in college and in life points to one thing over and over again: the kids who thrive are the ones who learned to handle things on their own while they still had a safety net. The kids who struggle are often the ones who never got the chance to fail small at home, so they fail big in the real world with no one around to help them recover. This book will show you how to be involved in a way that builds your kid up instead of making them dependent on you.

This book was written specifically for parents who feel like outsiders in this process. If you don't have a college degree yourself, if English isn't your first language, if you've never heard of the Common App or don't know what a "reach school" is, that's fine. Everything gets explained here from the ground up. No jargon. No assumptions. No moments where you're supposed to already know something that nobody ever taught you.

The families with money and connections have always had an advantage in college admissions. They hire counselors who know the system from the inside. They pay for essay coaches and interview prep. They have networks that open doors quietly, without anyone ever having to ask. This book can't give you those connections, but it can give you the knowledge. And knowledge used well closes the gap more than most people think.

The Big Idea — College Prep Is Life Prep

There's one idea at the center of everything in this book, and it's worth saying plainly right now so it can sit with you as you read.

Every single thing your child builds between 9th grade and 12th grade, every habit, every skill, every way of thinking about themselves and the world, will follow them into every job they ever have, every hard conversation they ever face, every setback they ever have to climb out of. The four years of high school aren't just a runway to college. They're the foundation for everything that comes after. And most parents, in the rush to check boxes and build a resume, completely miss that.

Think about what it actually takes to succeed in college. You have to manage your own time without anyone telling you what to do. You have to ask for help when you need it, which means you have to know yourself well enough to recognize when you're struggling. You have to handle rejection, conflict, and failure without falling apart. You have to figure out who you are when nobody from home is watching. Those aren't academic skills. They're life skills. And they don't appear magically on move-in day. They get built slowly, over four years of high school, if someone is paying attention.

Consider a typical parent, someone like Marco, a 46-year-old from El Salvador who's been working in construction management for twenty years and has a 16-year-old daughter who gets decent grades but has no idea what she wants to do with her life. Marco came here with nothing. His daughter has everything he didn't, a good school, stability, opportunities he could only dream about at her age. But Marco is terrified that she's coasting. That she doesn't feel the urgency he felt. That she'll drift through high school, get into some college, and come out the other side without a direction, without a plan, without the hunger that drove him.

What Marco doesn't realize yet is that his daughter's lack of direction isn't a character flaw. It's a developmental stage. And the college preparation process, when families understand how it actually works, can become one of the most powerful tools for helping a teenager build confidence, identity, resilience, and direction before adulthood arrives all at once. But to help your child navigate that process well, you first have to understand how dramatically the admissions landscape has changed — and why the old rules many parents still rely on no longer work the way they once did.

The college application asks your child to answer some of the hardest questions a person can face. Who are you? What matters to you? What have you done with what you've been given? What do you want to do with your life? Most teenagers have never been asked those questions directly. And most parents have never helped their kid think through them. This book will change that.

When you help your teenager build a college application, you're also helping them build an identity. When you help them write an essay about something that genuinely matters to them, you're teaching them how to reflect on their own experience and find meaning in it. When you help them push through a hard semester or recover from a bad grade, you're building the resilience that will carry them through every hard thing that comes after college. The acceptance letter is just one outcome. The young adult you raise in the process of getting there is the real result.

This book covers the full picture. You'll get the academic strategy, what courses to take, how GPA and rigor work together, and when test scores actually matter. You'll get the extracurricular strategy, not a list of clubs to join, but a real understanding of what colleges are looking for and how to help your child build a story instead of a resume. You'll get the financial strategy, how to find money, how to compare schools, and how to make a decision that doesn't saddle your family with debt for the next twenty years. You'll get the relationship strategy, how to stay close to your teenager through this process without making them feel controlled or suffocated. And you'll get the letting-go strategy, because the goal was never to get your child into college. The goal was always to raise someone who could handle what comes next.

That's what this book is really about.

Not the acceptance letter. Not the bumper sticker. Not the bragging rights at work on Monday morning. It's about raising a child who's genuinely ready for life. A kid who knows who they are, who can handle hard things, who shows up even when it's uncomfortable. Who doesn't need to be rescued every time something goes wrong. That kid exists in your house right now, in some form, in some stage of becoming. Your job over the next four years isn't to build a perfect application. Your job is to help that kid, your child, find themselves. This book will show you how.

Chapter 1
The Game Has Changed — What Modern College Admissions Actually Looks Like

Why the Old Rules Don't Work Anymore

Something shifted in college admissions over the last decade, and most parents have no idea it happened. The advice that worked for your generation, or even for older siblings just five or six years ahead of your teen, doesn't apply the same way anymore. And the parents who are still operating on those old assumptions are the ones getting blindsided when rejection letters start showing up.

The most dangerous belief out there right now is this one: if my kid gets good grades and joins a few clubs, they'll be fine.

That belief used to be mostly true. It isn't anymore.

UCLA received over 145,000 applications for its freshman class in 2023. The University of Michigan, which many families used to think of as a solid backup school, now admits fewer than 18% of applicants. Georgia Tech sits around 17%. Even schools that weren't particularly selective ten or fifteen years ago have seen their acceptance rates drop significantly as more students apply to more schools at once, thanks to the Common App making it easy to submit to fifteen or twenty schools with just a few extra clicks. The pool got bigger. The spots didn't.

That's the first thing you need to understand. The competition didn't just intensify at the Ivies. It changed almost everywhere.

Think about what that actually means for your child. A student who would have comfortably gotten into a well-regarded state school ten years ago might now sit in that school's "maybe" pile. Not because your child is less capable, but because the volume of applicants has exploded and admissions offices are making finer and finer distinctions between students who all look, on paper, pretty similar.

A few things happened at once, and they all compounded the problem. The Common Application went mainstream. Before it existed, applying to ten schools meant filling out ten separate applications, which was exhausting and expensive enough that most students applied to five or six schools at most. Now a student can add a new school to their list in under ten minutes. More applications per student means more applications per school, which means lower acceptance rates even if the school didn't change its standards at all.

At the same time, the COVID-19 pandemic pushed hundreds of schools to go test-optional, which had an unexpected side effect. Students who previously wouldn't have applied to certain schools because they felt their SAT or ACT scores weren't strong enough suddenly felt like they had a shot. So they applied. Many schools went test-optional as a temporary policy and ended up keeping it permanently. Schools that once used test scores as a natural filter no longer have that filter. Every application now requires a much deeper read.

The result is a system that's more competitive, more confusing, and more subjective than it's ever been. And if you're working with a mental model from ten years ago, or even five years ago, you're essentially reading a map of a city that's been completely rebuilt.

There's one more thing worth saying here, specifically for parents who didn't go through a four-year college admissions process themselves, or who went through it in another country. The American system is genuinely unusual. In many countries, admission is based almost entirely on one national exam. You score well, you get in. You don't, you don't. It's harsh, but it's clear. The American system doesn't work that way. It's layered, it's subjective, and it weighs a lot of different factors at once. That can feel deeply unfair, and sometimes it is. But it also means there are more ways to stand out than just a test score, and that's actually good news for your child if you know how to use it.

The action you need to take right now, before you read another word of this chapter, is to look up the current acceptance rates for the schools your child is interested in. Not the rates from five years ago. The current ones. Go to each school's official admissions page and find their most recent Common Data Set. It's a public document that every college is required to publish, and it shows you exactly how selective a school is, what the middle 50% of admitted students looked like in terms of GPA and test scores, and how many students applied versus how many got in. This one step will replace guesswork with real information, and it will change how you think about your child's list.

What 'Holistic Review' Really Means (And How to Use It to Your Advantage)

Every selective college says the same thing on their website: "We review applicants holistically." Most parents read that and nod, assuming it means they look at more than just grades. That's technically true, but it barely scratches the surface of what's actually happening when an admissions officer sits down with your child's file.

Holistic review is a structured process. It's not just a feeling.

Here's how it actually works at most selective schools. Each application gets read, often by two or more admissions officers. Those readers score or rate different parts of the application separately. Academic rating. Extracurricular rating. Essay rating. Sometimes a personal rating based on how the student comes across as a person across all the materials. These ratings get combined, discussed, and weighed against the school's priorities for that particular year's class. A school might need more students from the Midwest, or more engineers, or more first-generation college students to meet institutional goals. Your child's file doesn't exist in a vacuum. It gets evaluated against everyone else who applied that year, and against what the school is trying to build.

That sounds complicated because it is. But it also means the process is far more human than most parents realize.

The academic piece still matters enormously. GPA is the single most important factor in most applications, but it's not just the number. Admissions officers look at the rigor of the courses behind the number. A 3.7 earned in the most challenging classes your child's school offers tells a very different story than a 3.9 earned in the easiest possible schedule. They also look at the trend. A student whose grades improved steadily from 9th to 11th grade is more compelling than a student who peaked in 9th grade and slowly declined. The upward arc signals something real about character and growth. The downward arc raises questions.

Test scores, where they're still required or submitted, serve as a data point that helps admissions officers calibrate. They're not the deciding factor at most schools, but a strong score can push a borderline application over the line, and a very low score relative to a school's typical range can create doubt even for a strong student. The key word there is "relative." A 1200 SAT at a school where the middle 50% is 1050 to 1250 means something completely different than a 1200 at a school where the middle 50% is 1400 to 1550. Know the ranges for the specific schools on your child's list. That context is everything.

Essays are where many parents underestimate the stakes. An essay doesn't just show writing ability. It shows self-awareness. It shows whether a student can reflect on their own life and find something meaningful in it. Admissions officers read thousands of essays every cycle. They can tell almost immediately whether a student wrote something genuine or wrote what they thought the college wanted to hear. The essays that stand out aren't the ones about winning a championship or going on a mission trip. They're the ones where a real person comes through clearly on the page, someone with a specific voice, a specific perspective, and something real to say.

Recommendations matter more than most parents think, and less than some parents fear. In fact, some schools don't even require them because of how many applications they receive. But at schools that do consider or require them, a strong recommendation from a teacher who genuinely knows your child and can speak to specific qualities, specific moments, specific growth, carries real weight. A generic letter that could have been written for anyone in the class is essentially neutral. It doesn't hurt, but it doesn't help either. The goal is to have at least one teacher who can write about your child as an individual, not just as a student who got an A.

Demonstrated interest is a factor that flies completely under the radar for most families. Many schools track whether applicants have visited campus, attended virtual information sessions, opened emails, or interacted with the admissions office in any way. This data gets factored into decisions at schools that care about their yield rate, which is the percentage of admitted students who actually enroll. A school doesn't want to admit students who are going to say no. If your child is genuinely interested in a school, they should show it. Sign up for the mailing list. Attend a virtual event. Email the admissions office with a real question. Visit if it's financially possible. These actions cost almost nothing and can make a measurable difference.

The practical takeaway from all of this is that your child's application needs to tell a coherent story. Every part of it, the courses they took, the activities they chose, the essay they wrote, the way their recommender describes them, should point toward a consistent picture of who this person is. Not a perfect person. Not a superhuman. Just a real, specific, interesting person who has done something with their time and knows why it matters to them. That's the student who stands out in holistic review. Not the one with the longest list of activities. The one with the clearest sense of self.

Start working on this now by sitting down with your child and asking them one question: "If an admissions officer read everything about you, what would they think you care about most?" If your child can't answer that clearly, that's not a failure. It's information. It tells you exactly where to focus your energy over the next year or two. The goal is to get to a place where the answer is obvious, where everything in the application points to the same thing.

The Spike vs. the Well-Rounded Myth

Ask most parents what kind of student gets into a top college, and they'll describe the same kid. Good grades across every subject. Plays a sport. Does community service. Plays an instrument. Student council. Maybe some science fair or debate thrown in. Busy. Balanced. Well-rounded.

That kid exists at almost every high school in the country. And at selective colleges, that kid is extraordinarily hard to admit, because they look exactly like thousands of other applicants.

Admissions officers have a phrase they use internally: "Well-rounded students go to well-rounded classes." What they mean is that they're not trying to admit a class full of students who each did a little bit of everything. They're trying to build a class where each student brings something specific and deep. The violinist who's been performing since age seven. The kid who started a small business and can talk about what they learned when it failed. The teenager who has been obsessed with marine biology since middle school and spent two summers doing research at a local university. Each of those students has a spike. One area where they developed real expertise or commitment, and can speak about it with genuine knowledge and passion.

A spike isn't just an activity. It's a signal.

It tells an admissions officer that this student knows how to commit to something. That they can sustain interest and effort over time. That they've developed actual skills, not just a list of things they showed up for. And perhaps most importantly, it tells a story about who this person is and what they might contribute to a campus community. Colleges aren't just admitting students. They're building communities. They want the student who's going to run the robotics club, or start a new literary magazine, or bring a perspective to the classroom that nobody else has.

Think about Priya, a hypothetical 16-year-old whose parents immigrated from India and who has been quietly building something unusual since 8th grade. She got interested in food insecurity after a school project and started volunteering at a local food bank. Over time she started noticing patterns in which families came in and when. She began researching food deserts in her city. By 10th grade she'd started a small initiative connecting local restaurants with the food bank to donate surplus meals. She's not a straight-A student. She got a B in chemistry. She doesn't play a sport. But she has a spike that runs through everything in her application, a genuine, sustained, evolving commitment to one specific problem that she can speak about with real depth. That application tells a story. A college reading it doesn't just see a student. They see a future contributor.

This is a hypothetical scenario, but it reflects exactly the kind of profile—such as demonstrated leadership, unique extracurricular involvement, or academic excellence—that stands out in modern admissions.

The well-rounded myth is particularly hard to let go of for parents who grew up being told that a balanced, versatile student is the goal. And to be fair, balance isn't bad. Your child shouldn't drop everything that doesn't relate to their spike. A student who plays soccer and does theater and also has a deep passion for environmental advocacy is fine. The problem is when parents push their kids to add more and more activities for the sake of having a longer list, without any of it going anywhere meaningful.

Depth beats breadth. Every time.

Here's how to help your child find their spike if they don't have one yet. Ask them what they'd do with their time if grades and college applications didn't exist. What do they actually enjoy? What makes them lose track of time? What problems in the world genuinely bother them? What could they talk about for an hour without getting bored? The answers to those questions point toward something true. Your job isn't to turn that thing into a resume item. Your job is to help them go deeper into it. Sign them up for a related course. Find a local organization working on that issue. Look for a summer program or internship in that space. Help them do more of the thing they already care about, and the spike builds itself naturally over time.

One more thing worth saying here. The spike doesn't have to be glamorous or prestigious. It doesn't have to be research at a university or a nonprofit with a fancy name. A student who worked 20 hours a week at a grocery store to help their family, and who can write about what they learned from that, has a spike. A student who taught themselves to code and built a simple app for their neighborhood has a spike. A student who cared for a younger sibling while their parent worked nights and who can reflect on what that responsibility taught them has a spike. Admissions officers are human beings. They recognize real life when they see it. Don't let anyone tell you that your child's story isn't impressive enough just because it doesn't come with a trophy.

Public vs. Private, Reach vs. Safety — Building a Smart College List

One of the biggest mistakes families make in this process has nothing to do with grades or essays. It's the list itself. Applying to the wrong schools, or applying to the right schools in the wrong proportions, is one of the most common and most fixable problems in college admissions.

I'm sure some of you reading this are parents of what school staff often call "high flyers" — students with near-perfect grades, strong test scores, and impressive extracurriculars. These students are often encouraged to apply primarily to highly selective schools with extremely low (3% or less) acceptance rates. Having a dream school is fine. Applying to a few highly selective schools is fine. But the key is building a balanced list, not one built entirely around lottery-level admissions odds.

So what do I mean by a balanced list? I mean a college list that has three types of schools: reach schools, match schools, and safety schools. Most parents (and students) know these terms. Far fewer actually build a list that uses them correctly.

A reach school is one where your child's GPA and test scores fall below the school's middle 50% range, or where the acceptance rate is low enough that even strong applicants get rejected regularly. These are schools where admission is genuinely uncertain, even for a well-qualified student. It's fine to have two or three reaches on a list. It's not fine to have a list that's mostly reaches with one or two schools tacked on at the bottom as afterthoughts.

A match school is one where your child's academic profile falls comfortably within the school's admitted student range, and where they have a realistic chance of admission. Not a guaranteed chance, but a real one. This is where the bulk of the list should live, roughly half of the schools your child applies to.

A safety school is one where your child is clearly above the school's typical admitted student profile, where admission is as close to certain as anything in this process gets, and where your child would genuinely be happy to attend. That last part is critical. A safety school is not a punishment school. It's not a fallback your child would be embarrassed to go to. If your child wouldn't be okay going there, it's not a real safety. It's just a school you applied to for psychological comfort.

The public versus private question trips up a lot of families, especially those who are watching costs closely. The assumption is that public schools are cheaper and private schools are expensive. That's often true for in-state students at public universities, but it's not always true once financial aid enters the picture. Many private colleges have large endowments and offer substantial need-based aid that can bring the actual cost below what a public university would charge. Some private schools meet 100% of demonstrated financial need. Some don't come close. You can't know which category a school falls into without looking at the numbers for your specific family situation.

The other thing the public versus private question often misses is fit. A large public university with 50,000 students is a fundamentally different experience from a small private liberal arts college with 2,000 students. Neither is better in the abstract. But for a specific kid with a specific personality and specific goals, one might be dramatically better than the other. A student who thrives in small class settings with lots of faculty interaction might struggle at a huge state school where introductory classes have 300 people and professors don't learn your name until junior year. A student who wants a vibrant social scene, a wide range of majors to explore, and a big campus energy might feel suffocated at a tiny school where everyone knows everyone by October.

Name recognition is one of the worst ways to evaluate a college, and it's one of the most common. A school that your coworker has heard of is not automatically better than a school they haven't. What actually matters is whether the school has a strong program in the area your child wants to study, whether the school's graduates get the kinds of jobs your child is interested in, whether the school's culture and size match how your child learns and lives, and whether the school's actual cost after financial aid makes sense for your family. Those four questions will tell you more about whether a school is right than any ranking ever will.

To build a smart list, start with twelve to fifteen schools total. Aim for roughly two to three reaches, six to eight matches, and three to four genuine safeties. For each school, look up three things: the acceptance rate, the middle 50% GPA and test score range for admitted students, and the average financial aid package for families at your income level. That last number is usually available on the school's net price calculator, which every college is required to have on their website. Spend an hour doing this research before your child writes a single word of any application. It will save you months of wasted effort.

Timelines, Deadlines, and Decision Types — The Vocabulary You Need to Know

If you've ever sat across from another parent at a school event and nodded along while they talked about Early Decision binding agreements and Regular Decision pools, not wanting to admit you had no idea what they meant, this section is for you. These terms matter. Getting them wrong can cost your child real opportunities, or lock your family into a financial commitment you weren't prepared for.

Early Decision, almost always called ED, is a binding agreement. Your child applies to one school early, usually with a November 1st or November 15th deadline, and if they're admitted, they are committed to attending. They must withdraw all other applications and accept the offer, usually within a few weeks. The advantage is real: acceptance rates in the ED round are often significantly higher than in the regular round at the same school, because colleges love students who have declared them their first choice. The risk is also real: if the financial aid offer isn't what your family needs, getting out of an ED commitment is difficult and requires documenting genuine financial hardship. For families who need to compare financial aid packages before committing, Early Decision is a high-risk move. For families where cost is less of a concern and the school is a clear first choice, it can be a genuine strategic advantage.

Early Action, called EA, is non-binding. Your child applies early and gets an answer early, usually by mid-December, but they don't have to commit until the regular May 1st deadline. This is almost always a good move if your child's application is ready. There's no downside to getting an answer earlier, and some schools have slightly higher acceptance rates in the EA round. Some schools offer Restrictive Early Action, sometimes called Single Choice Early Action, which means your child can apply early to that school but can't apply early anywhere else. Harvard, Yale, Princeton, and Stanford use this model. Read the fine print carefully.

Regular Decision is the standard round. Applications are typically due January 1st or January 15th, and decisions come out in late March or early April. This is where the majority of applicants land, and it's the most competitive round at schools that also offer ED and EA, because the students who were most committed to those schools already applied early. That doesn't mean Regular Decision is a losing strategy. For students who need more time to strengthen their application, or who want to compare financial aid packages from multiple schools before deciding, it's absolutely the right choice.

Rolling admissions works differently from all of the above. Schools with rolling admissions review applications as they come in and send decisions on a continuous basis, rather than holding all applications until a specific date. The practical implication is significant: applying early in a rolling admissions cycle gives your child a real advantage, because there are more spots available at the start of the cycle than at the end. Many large public universities use rolling admissions. If a school on your child's list uses this model, don't wait until January to apply. Submit in September or October if the application is ready.

There's one more term worth knowing: waitlist. Being waitlisted means the school hasn't admitted your child, but hasn't rejected them either. They're holding them in case admitted students decline their offers. Waitlist outcomes vary enormously from school to school and year to year. Some schools take hundreds of students off the waitlist. Some take none. If your child is waitlisted at a school they genuinely want to attend, they should send a letter of continued interest that updates the school on anything new since they applied and reaffirms their commitment to attend if admitted. They should also move forward with their other options and not put their life on hold waiting for a waitlist decision that may never come.

The strategic use of these timelines is something most families never think about. They treat deadlines as things to scramble toward rather than tools to use deliberately. A student who applies Early Action to several schools they're genuinely excited about, uses the resulting decisions to understand where they stand academically, and then makes a thoughtful Regular Decision or Early Decision II choice in January is using the calendar as a strategy. That's a very different position than a student who submits everything on January 1st and spends four months waiting anxiously for answers.

Your action here is specific. Sit down with your child and map out every school on their list with the corresponding deadline and decision type. Write it on a physical calendar or put it in a shared digital calendar that both of you can see. For each school, note whether it's ED, EA, Restrictive EA, Regular Decision, or Rolling. Then work backward from each deadline to figure out when the application needs to be complete. Essays take longer than anyone expects. Recommendations need to be requested weeks in advance. Test scores need to be sent officially, which takes time. Build in buffer. The families who miss deadlines or submit rushed applications in the final hours are almost always the ones who treated the deadlines as the starting line instead of the finish line.

What We Covered and Your Next Steps

This chapter covered a lot of ground, and all of it was intentional. Before you can make good decisions about your child's college process, you need an accurate picture of what you're actually dealing with. Not the picture from ten years ago. Not the picture from other parents' stories. The real one.

The admissions landscape is more competitive than it's ever been, and that competition extends well beyond the schools everyone has heard of. Holistic review is a real process with real structure, and every part of your child's application either adds to or detracts from the story it tells. The well-rounded student myth is one of the most persistent and most damaging ideas in college prep, and the sooner you let go of it, the sooner your child can start building something that actually stands out. The college list itself is a strategic tool, not just a wish list, and building it thoughtfully changes everything that comes after. And the application calendar, used deliberately, gives your family real options instead of just deadlines to survive.

These aren't just admissions insights. Every one of them connects to something bigger. A child who learns to tell a coherent story about who they are and what they care about doesn't just write a better college essay. They walk into every job interview, every relationship, and every hard conversation with that same clarity. A child who learns to go deep on something they genuinely love doesn't just impress an admissions officer. They build the kind of focused commitment that makes people successful over a lifetime. The college process, done right, is the training ground for all of it.

Here are your specific next steps for this week:

First, look up the current acceptance rates and Common Data Sets for every school your child has mentioned wanting to attend. Get the real numbers in front of you so your planning is based on facts.

Second, ask your child the spike question: "What would you do with your time if college applications didn't exist?" Write down whatever they say without judgment. You're gathering information, not making decisions.

Third, pull up the net price calculator on the website of two or three schools your child is interested in. Enter your family's income and household information. Look at the estimated cost after aid. Let that number inform how you think about the list.

Fourth, create a simple document with every school your child is considering, the deadline type, and the application due date. Share it with your teenager. Make it something you both can see and update together.

None of these steps take more than a few hours total. But they will change the quality of every conversation you have about college from this point forward. That's the difference between reacting to this process and actually running it.

Chapter 2
The 9th Grade Foundation – Building Habits That Will Last a Lifetime

Why 9th Grade Is the Most Underestimated Year in High School

Most parents don't start paying close attention until 11th grade. That's when the PSAT scores come back, when the school counselor starts mentioning college fairs, when other parents at pickup start talking about AP, IB classes and summer programs. It feels like 11th grade is when the real work begins.

By then, half the transcript is already written.

Every grade your child earns in 9th grade goes into their GPA. Every class they choose, every habit they form, every pattern they establish in that first year of high school becomes part of the permanent record that admissions officers will read three years later. There's no completely erasing it, no averaging it out, no footnote explaining that they hadn't figured things out yet. The transcript tells the story from day one, and 9th grade is the first chapter.

This matters more than most parents realize, and the numbers back it up. When admissions officers talk about academic trajectory, they mean the shape of a student's grades over four years. A student who starts strong in 9th grade and stays strong sends a clear signal: this person can handle increasing pressure and keep showing up. A student who struggles in 9th grade and improves dramatically by 11th grade has a better story than one who peaked early and drifted, but they're still fighting an uphill battle because those early grades are already in the file. The student who never had to fight that battle at all, because they built the right habits from the start, has the cleanest path of all three.

There's something else happening in 9th grade that has nothing to do with GPA. Your child is forming an identity as a student. Not just whether they're "good at school" or not, but how they respond to difficulty, how they handle a teacher they don't like, how they manage their time when nobody is standing over them, how they bounce back after a bad test. These patterns get set early. A student who learns in 9th grade that struggling on something doesn't mean they're stupid, that asking for help is smart, and that consistent effort matters more than natural talent, that student carries those beliefs into every hard class, every tough semester, and every challenging situation for the rest of their life.

A student who learns the opposite in 9th grade, that school is something that happens to you, that grades are mostly about luck or talent, that the goal is just to get through it, carries those beliefs too.

Think about a parent like Fatima, a 41-year-old who came to the United States from Nigeria when she was 22. She works as a home health aide and has a 14-year-old son named Daniel who just started high school. Fatima didn't go through the American school system herself. She doesn't know what a GPA calculation looks like or how freshman year grades factor into a college application. She reasonably assumed that 9th grade was a warm-up year. That's what her coworker told her. That's what it felt like from the outside, since Daniel seemed to have less homework than she expected. So she didn't push. She figured there was time. By the time she found out that Daniel had gotten a C in English and a D on his first history test, the semester was nearly over. She scrambled, got him a tutor, and he finished the year with a 2.8 GPA. He's a smart kid. He's capable. But now his 9th grade year is on the record, and every year after this, he'll be working to show an upward trend instead of just building on a solid start. This is a hypothetical scenario, but it's one that plays out constantly, in every kind of family, for the exact same reason: nobody told them that 9th grade was the moment to pay attention.

You're reading this now, which means you know. That's the whole point.

If your child is already in 9th grade, the most important thing you can do right now is check in on where they stand academically, not to panic, but to get an accurate picture. Log into whatever parent portal your school uses and look at current grades in every class. Not just the final grade, but the individual assignments. Are there missing assignments? Are there patterns, like consistently low quiz scores in one class? Are there subjects where they're clearly thriving? This information tells you where to focus your energy. You're not looking for perfection. You're looking for early warning signs you can address now, while there's still time in the semester to change the outcome.

If your child hasn't started 9th grade yet, you're in the best possible position. You can help them walk in with a plan instead of figuring it out after the fact. The sections that follow in this chapter will give you exactly what you need to do that.

One more thing worth saying here, especially for parents who are worried their child already made a rough start. A difficult 9th grade year is not the end of the story. Colleges do look at trends, and a student who stumbles in 9th grade and then builds three years of strong, consistent performance has a compelling arc. The stumble becomes part of the narrative, evidence of growth rather than evidence of failure. But that only works if the student actually turns it around, and turning it around requires building the habits we're going to cover right now.

The Three Habits That Separate Thriving Students from Struggling Ones

Raw intelligence doesn't determine whether a student succeeds in high school. It helps, but it's not the deciding factor. The students who thrive, the ones who finish four years with strong grades, meaningful activities, and a real sense of direction, almost always share three specific habits. And the students who struggle, even the smart ones, almost always lack them.

These habits aren't complicated. But they don't develop on their own.

The first habit is managing time intentionally. Not just being busy, not just having a schedule, but making deliberate choices about when to do what, and following through on those choices without someone else enforcing them. This sounds basic. It's not. Most 14-year-olds have never had to manage their own time in any real way. Elementary and middle school are structured environments where adults tell them where to be and when. High school shifts that responsibility, and college shifts it even further. A student who hasn't built this skill by the time they leave home is going to struggle in ways that have nothing to do with how smart they are.

Here's how to help your child build this habit without turning it into a daily battle. Start with one simple tool: a weekly planning session. Every Sunday evening, sit down together for 15 minutes, not to lecture, just to plan. Look at the week ahead. What assignments are due? What tests are coming? What activities or commitments are on the calendar? Remind them that hanging out with a friend is an activity and they need to plan for it to get a clear picture of their week. Write it all down in one place, whether that's a paper planner, a notes app, or a shared Google calendar. Then help your child identify two or three specific windows during the week when they'll do their work. Not "sometime after school." Specific times: Tuesday from 4 to 5:30, Thursday from 6 to 7:30. The act of writing it down and committing to a time is the habit. Over a few weeks, it becomes automatic.

The goal here isn't to micromanage your child's schedule. It's to help them build the internal structure that lets them manage themselves. Once the habit is in place, you step back. You stop reminding them. You let them own it. If they miss something, that's a learning moment, not a crisis. A missed assignment in 9th grade that teaches a student to plan better is worth far more in the long run than a parent who caught it before it happened and robbed them of the lesson.

The second habit is taking ownership of their own learning. This one is harder to teach, and it's the one most likely to cause friction between parents and teenagers. Taking ownership means your child doesn't wait to be told what to do. They notice when they don't understand something and they seek help. They talk to their teacher before the test, not after the grade comes back. They ask questions in class even when it feels awkward. They take responsibility for their results instead of blaming the teacher, the test, or the fact that the class is boring.

This habit doesn't develop because you told your child to have it. It develops when your child has the experience of advocating for themselves and seeing it work. So your job is to create those experiences deliberately. When your child gets a grade they're unhappy with, don't immediately email the teacher yourself. Instead, ask your child: "What do you think happened? What would you do differently? Have you thought about talking to the teacher?" Then help them figure out what to say. Practice it with them if they're nervous. Let them send the email or have the conversation themselves, with your coaching beforehand if needed. The outcome of that specific situation matters less than the skill they're building by doing it themselves.

For immigrant and working-class families, this habit carries extra weight. Many students from these backgrounds have been taught, correctly in many contexts, that you don't question authority, that you keep your head down, that you don't ask for more than what you're given. Those values have real wisdom in certain situations. But in an American academic environment, the student who advocates for themselves, who talks to professors, who asks for extensions when life gets hard, who shows up to office hours, that student gets more help, more opportunities, and better outcomes. Teaching your child to advocate for themselves in school is teaching them to advocate for themselves in every workplace, every negotiation, and every difficult situation they'll face as an adult.

The third habit is recovering quickly from setbacks. This one might be the most important of the three, and it's the one that's hardest for parents to stay out of. Every student in high school is going to fail at something. A test they studied hard for and still bombed. A project they worked on that got a lower grade than they expected. A class where they just can't seem to get traction no matter what they do. A rejection from a club or a team or a program they wanted. These things happen to every student, including the ones who end up at great colleges.

The difference between thriving students and struggling ones isn't whether they experience setbacks. It's how long they stay down after one.

A student who gets a bad grade and spirals, who decides they're bad at the subject, who gives up on that class and starts coasting, is learning a pattern that will follow them everywhere. A student who gets a bad grade, feels disappointed for a day, figures out what went wrong, and adjusts their approach is building resilience in real time. That resilience is what gets people through hard semesters in college, through job losses, through failed relationships, through every difficult thing life throws at them.

Your role in building this habit is mostly about what you don't do. Don't rush to fix the problem for them. Don't call the school before your child has had a chance to process what happened. Don't tell them the grade doesn't matter when it does. Instead, let them feel the disappointment, sit with it briefly, and then ask the forward-facing question: "Okay, so what's the plan from here?" That question, asked consistently and without blame, teaches your child that setbacks are temporary and that the next move is always available. That belief is one of the most valuable things you can give them.

How to Have the 'College Conversation' Without Your Teen Shutting Down

You know the look. You bring up college, or grades, or the future, and something in your teenager's face just closes. The eye roll. The one-word answers. The sudden need to be somewhere else. You're not imagining it. That shutdown is real, and it happens for a specific reason.

Most college conversations feel like evaluations. Your teen hears the word "college" and what registers is: you're not doing enough, you're behind, I'm worried about you, and this is a problem. Even when that's not what you mean, it's often what they hear. And when people feel like they're being assessed and found lacking, they shut down. That's not a teenager thing. That's a human thing.

The goal isn't to stop talking about college. The goal is to change what those conversations feel like.

Start by changing the timing. Conversations about college don't belong at the dinner table when everyone is tired, or right after your child gets home from school, or immediately after you see a grade you're unhappy with. Those moments are loaded. The best conversations happen when things are already relaxed, when you're in the car together, when you're doing something side by side, when there's no eye contact required and no sense that this is a formal meeting. The car is genuinely one of the best places for hard conversations with teenagers. They can't walk away, there's no face-to-face pressure, and the forward motion of driving creates a subtle sense of momentum that makes talking easier.

Change the framing next. Instead of starting with college as a destination, start with your child as a person. The question "What schools are you thinking about?" puts pressure on them to have answers they probably don't have yet. The question "What's something you've been really into lately?" opens a door without any pressure behind it. From there, you can build naturally. "That's interesting, have you ever thought about what it would look like to do more of that?" Then, much later, "I wonder if there are programs that focus on that kind of thing." You're not hiding the college conversation. You're arriving at it through genuine curiosity about your child, which is a completely different experience for them.

There's a specific script worth having in your back pocket for the first real college conversation. It goes something like this: "I want to talk about the next few years, not because I'm worried or because I think you're behind, but because I want us to figure this out together. I don't want to be the parent who's pushing you toward something without asking what you actually want. So I'm asking. What do you want the next four years to look like?" Then stop talking. Let them answer. Whatever they say, even if it's "I don't know," that's valuable information and it's a starting point, not a failure.

The phrase "I don't know" from a teenager about their future is almost always honest, not lazy. Most 14 and 15-year-olds genuinely don't know what they want. They're not supposed to. The job of the next four years is partly to figure that out. When your child says, "I don't know," the right response isn't to fill in the blank for them. It's to say, "That's completely fine. Part of what the next few years are for is figuring that out. So let's just keep paying attention to what you enjoy and what you're good at, and we'll figure out the rest as we go." That response takes the pressure off and signals that you're a safe person to think out loud with.

For parents who are immigrants or who didn't go to college themselves, these conversations carry extra emotional weight. You may have sacrificed enormously to give your child this opportunity. You may feel like you can't afford for them to be casual about it. That feeling is valid. But when that weight comes through in the conversation, when your child can feel the pressure of your sacrifice and your fear behind every question you ask, it becomes a burden they carry rather than a conversation they're part of. You can honor your sacrifice and still give your child the space to find their own motivation. In fact, that's the only way it works. A teenager who works hard because they're afraid of disappointing you will stop working the moment they're out of your house. A teenager who works hard because they've found something they genuinely care about will keep going long after you're not watching.

One practical thing you can do this week: send your child a text, not a conversation, just a text with one low-stakes question about something they're interested in. Not about school. Not about grades. Something like: "Hey, I heard there's a documentary about [thing they mentioned liking]. Want to watch it this weekend?" That's it. You're building the channel of communication before you need it for harder conversations. The parents who can talk to their teenagers about college are almost always the ones who've been talking to their teenagers about everything else first.

Extracurriculars in 9th Grade — Exploration, Not Resume Building

There's a version of 9th grade extracurricular planning that looks very organized and feels very productive and is actually doing your child real harm. It goes like this: you sit down with a list of activities that "look good" for college applications, you identify the ones your child can reasonably fit into their schedule, and you sign them up. Chess club. Debate. Volunteer hours at the hospital. Maybe a sport. The calendar fills up. The resume starts to take shape. And your child is miserable, going through the motions of activities they never chose, building a profile that looks impressive to no one because admissions officers have been reading these profiles for years and they can tell the difference between a student who's genuinely engaged and one who's checking boxes.

9th grade is not the time to build a resume. It's the time to find out what your child actually cares about.

That sounds simple, but it runs directly against the instinct most parents have when they feel behind. When you're worried your child isn't doing enough, adding activities feels like taking action. And taking action feels better than waiting. But the wrong activities, pursued for the wrong reasons, don't just waste time. They crowd out the space your child needs to stumble onto something they actually love. You can't find your passion on a schedule someone else built for you.

The research on what makes college applications stand out points consistently to one thing: authentic, sustained engagement. Not the number of activities. Not the prestige of the organizations. Whether the student genuinely cared about what they were doing and whether they stuck with it long enough to go somewhere with it. A student who spent three years deeply involved in one thing they chose themselves, who grew in that thing, who took on more responsibility over time, who can talk about it with real knowledge and genuine feeling, that student is more compelling than one who has twelve activities and can't speak meaningfully about any of them.

So what does exploration actually look like in practice? It means saying yes to things your child is curious about, even if they don't seem impressive. It means letting them try something and quit if it's not right, without making that feel like failure. It means asking "what did you think of that?" instead of "is that something you could put on a college application?" It means paying attention to what your child talks about with energy and what they do willingly versus what they have to be pushed toward. Those observations are data. They're telling you something real about who your child is and what they might want to pursue more seriously.

The early signs of a "spike" almost never look like a spike at first. They look like a kid who keeps bringing up the same topic at dinner. A kid who spends their free time watching videos about something specific. A kid who gets genuinely frustrated by a problem in their community and keeps thinking about it. A kid who finds one class interesting in a way that's different from the others. These are seeds. Your job in 9th grade isn't to water all of them equally. It's to notice which ones your child keeps coming back to on their own, and then find low-commitment ways to let them explore that thing more deeply.

Low-commitment matters here. Don't sign your child up for a year-long commitment to something they've never tried. Look for a six-week class, a one-day workshop, a local club meeting, a volunteer shift, a summer program that's a week long. Give them a taste before they decide if they want more. This approach respects their developing sense of self and builds the habit of trying new things without the pressure of being locked in.

There's a specific conversation worth having with your 9th grader about extracurriculars, and it goes like this. Sit down together and make two lists. The first list is everything they're currently doing outside of class. The second list is everything they've ever been curious about but haven't tried. Then look at both lists together and ask: "Is there anything on the second list you'd want to explore this year?" Let them choose. You're not approving or disapproving. You're creating the conditions for them to make a real choice about their own time. That act of choosing, and then following through on the choice, is itself a skill they're building. It's the beginning of self-direction, which is one of the most valuable things a college application can show and one of the most important things a person can have in adult life.

For parents who feel pressure from their community, whether that's other immigrant families where every child seems to be doing advanced everything, or competitive school environments where it feels like everyone else's kid already has a plan, this is worth saying clearly: the student who goes deep on something genuine will consistently outperform the student who goes wide on things that look good. Every single time. Not because the admissions process rewards authenticity as a concept, but because genuine engagement produces real skills, real stories, and real conviction that comes through in every part of an application. You can't fake that. And you don't need to, if you start building it now.

What to Do This Month — Your 9th Grade Action Plan

Everything covered in this chapter points to the same truth: 9th grade is where the foundation gets built, and the foundation determines everything that comes after. Not just the college application. The habits your child builds now, how they manage their time, how they respond to difficulty, how they talk about themselves and their future, those habits go everywhere with them. Into college. Into their first job. Into every hard thing they'll face when you're not there to help.

The following steps are specific. Each one has a clear action and a clear outcome. Work through them in order over the next four weeks.

In week one, do a transcript check-in. Log into your school's parent portal and pull up your child's current grades in every class. Don't react out loud to what you see. Just gather the information. Write down any class where your child has a grade below a B, any missing assignments, and any subject where there seems to be a pattern of low scores. Then schedule a 20-minute conversation with your child, not a lecture, a conversation, where you share what you saw and ask them what's going on in each of those classes. Your goal is to understand, not to fix. Ask questions. Listen to the answers. At the end, pick one specific thing to address together, whether that's getting a tutor, reaching out to a teacher, or adjusting the study schedule.

In week two, introduce the weekly planning session. Pick a consistent time, Sunday evening works well for most families, and spend 15 minutes together looking at the week ahead. Write down every assignment, test, and commitment. Help your child identify specific time blocks for studying. Keep it short, keep it calm, and keep the focus on planning rather than evaluating. Do this every week for a month. By the end of the month, your child should be able to run the session themselves with minimal prompting from you.

In week three, have the exploration conversation about extracurriculars. Use the two-list approach described earlier in this chapter. Make the first list of current activities. Make the second list of things they've been curious about. Then ask your child to pick one thing from the second list to try in some low-commitment form before the end of the school year. Help them find one specific opportunity, a club meeting, a class, a workshop, a volunteer shift, and put it on the calendar. Don't pick it for them. Help them find it themselves.

In week four, have the first college conversation using the low-pressure script from the earlier section. Do it in the car if possible. Start with curiosity about your child, not with college as the topic. Ask what they've been enjoying, what's been hard, what they've been thinking about. Let the conversation go where it goes. If college comes up naturally, great. If it doesn't, that's fine too. The goal of this first conversation is just to open the channel, to establish that you and your child can talk about the future without it turning into a stressful event. That channel will matter enormously over the next three years.

None of these steps require money. None of them require a private counselor or a special program. They require your time, your attention, and your willingness to show up as a parent who's paying close attention during a year when most parents aren't. That's the whole advantage. The families who start in 9th grade with intention don't just end up with better college applications. They end up with teenagers who know how to manage themselves, who can advocate for their own needs, who recover from hard things without falling apart, and who have a genuine sense of what they care about. That's not just a college outcome. That's a life outcome. And it starts right now.

Chapter 3
10th Grade – Finding the Thread and Going Deeper

Sophomore year has a reputation for being the quiet middle child of high school. Not the nervous excitement of freshman year, not the high-stakes pressure of junior year. Just... the middle. A lot of parents treat it that way too, checking in less, assuming things are on track, waiting for the moment when college prep "really" starts.

That's a costly mistake.

10th grade is actually one of the most important years in the entire four-year stretch, not because of any single deadline or test, but because of what's possible right now that won't be possible later. Your child is old enough to start thinking seriously about who they are and what they care about. They're young enough that there's still time to create something meaningful before the pressure of applications really sets in. The window between those two things is sophomore year, and the families who use it well arrive at junior year with a clear direction, a developing story, and a teenager who feels like they're moving toward something instead of just surviving school.

This chapter is about how to use that window on purpose.

From Exploration to Direction — Helping Your Child Find Their 'Thing'

In 9th grade, the goal was exploration. Try things. See what sticks. Pay attention to what your child keeps coming back to on their own. That was the right approach for freshman year, and hopefully you used it well. But 10th grade asks something different. The wide-open phase needs to start narrowing. Not into a rigid plan, but into a direction. A thread. Something that connects the dots between what your child enjoys, what they're good at, and what they might want to do more of.

Finding that thread early is the difference between a college application that feels alive and one that feels assembled.

Here's what the thread actually looks like in practice. It's not a career plan. Your 15-year-old doesn't need to know what they want to do for the rest of their life. The thread is simpler than that. It's a pattern of genuine interest that shows up consistently across different parts of their life. The kid who loves biology class and also volunteers at an animal shelter and also spends time watching nature documentaries on their own time has a thread, even if they haven't named it yet. The kid who's always been the one in the friend group who notices when someone is struggling, who naturally mediates conflicts, and who chose peer counseling as an elective has a thread. Your job in 10th grade is to help your child see that thread, name it, and start pulling on it deliberately.

The tricky part is separating what your child cares about from what they're doing to please you or to look good on paper. This distinction matters enormously, because admissions officers read thousands of applications every year and they've gotten very good at spotting the difference. An essay written about a genuine passion has a different energy than one written about an activity the student added to their schedule because someone told them it would help their application. You can feel it when you read it. So can they.

Ask yourself honestly: are the activities your child is currently doing things they chose, or things that got chosen for them? Are they talking about any of these things outside of the context of school or applications? Do they bring them up at dinner without being asked? Do they seem honestly energized after doing them, or just relieved that it's done? These are not trick questions. They're diagnostic ones. The answers tell you whether you're building something real or building a facade that will eventually feel hollow to everyone who reads it.

Here's a specific exercise to do with your child this month. Set aside 30 minutes on a weekend when neither of you is rushed. Bring a piece of paper and two pens. Ask your child to answer these four questions out loud while you write down what they say, without editing or commenting:

One: What's something you've done in the last year that made you lose track of time? Two: What problem in the world, your school, your neighborhood, or anywhere, genuinely bothers you? Three: What's something you know more about than most people your age? Four: What would you do differently with your time if grades and applications didn't exist?

Don't rush through this. Let them think. Let there be silence. When they're done, read back what you wrote. Then ask one follow-up question: "Is there anything on this list that you'd want to do more of?" Whatever they point to, that's the thread. Not a finished plan. A starting point. Your next job is to help them find one concrete way to go deeper into that thing before the school year ends.

Going deeper doesn't mean adding a prestigious program or an expensive summer experience. It means finding the next level of engagement with something they already care about. If they love cooking, it means looking for a local culinary workshop or a food-focused volunteer opportunity, not enrolling in a professional program. If they're interested in social justice, it means finding one local organization doing that work and asking if a high schooler can help, not starting a nonprofit from scratch. The depth comes from consistent, real engagement over time. Not from the name of the thing on a resume.

One more thing worth saying here, especially for parents who are quietly hoping their child will choose a direction that feels safe or prestigious. The thread your child finds may not be the one you'd pick for them. It may not be pre-med or pre-law or anything that comes with a clear, recognizable career path. It might be something you don't fully understand or something that doesn't sound like a stable future from where you're standing. Before you redirect them, consider this: a student who is genuinely passionate about something unusual and can speak about it with depth and conviction is more compelling to a college admissions officer than a student who is mildly interested in something conventional. Passion is visible. Authenticity is visible. And a kid who knows what they care about and why is already ahead of most of their peers, regardless of what that thing actually is.

Academics in 10th Grade — When to Push and When to Back Off

Sophomore year is when course rigor starts to matter in a way it didn't quite yet in 9th grade. Admissions officers look at the full four-year academic picture, and by the end of 10th grade, your child will have half their high school transcript on record. The courses they choose this year, and the grades they earn in them, are part of that permanent picture.

But there's a version of "rigor" that helps your child and a version that hurts them, and the difference is worth understanding clearly.

Rigor means taking challenging courses relative to what your child's school offers and relative to what your child is actually ready to handle. It does not mean loading up on every AP or honors class available because more always looks better. It doesn't. A student who takes four AP classes in 10th grade and earns Bs and Cs in all of them has a weaker academic story than a student who takes two AP classes they're genuinely prepared for and earns As in both, along with strong grades in their other courses. Admissions officers understand the difference between a student who challenged themselves appropriately and a student who overreached and got buried.

The question to ask before adding any advanced course to your child's schedule is this: does my child have the foundation for this class, and do they have the bandwidth for it given everything else in their life right now? Both parts of that question matter equally. A student who is academically ready for AP Chemistry but is also carrying a part-time job, a demanding extracurricular, and a family responsibility at home may not have the bandwidth to do that class justice. Adding it anyway doesn't show ambition. It shows poor planning, and the grade reflects that.

For example, let's consider a parent named Julie. She is 43 years old and works as a medical billing specialist. Julie has a 15-year-old daughter named Paula. As a single mom, she has worked incredibly hard to provide Paula with opportunities she never had.

When Paula's school counselor mentioned that AP World History was available in 10th grade, Julie pushed hard for Paula to take it. Paula is a solid student, mostly Bs with some As, but she's also heavily involved in her school's dance program, which takes up three afternoons a week. By October of sophomore year, Paula was drowning. The AP class required a level of reading and essay writing she hadn't fully developed yet, and she didn't have the time to catch up. Her grade dropped to a C, which pulled her GPA down and shook her confidence in a way that took months to recover from. Julie's instinct came from love and from a deep understanding that opportunity matters. But the outcome hurt Paula's transcript and, more importantly, hurt how she felt about herself as a student. This is a hypothetical scenario, but it reflects a pattern that plays out in families across every income level and background.

The right approach to course selection in 10th grade is a conversation, not a decision you make for your child. Sit down with your child and their current transcript. Look at where they're strongest and where they've struggled. Then look at the courses available for next year and ask: which of these genuinely interests you, and which do you feel ready for? If there's a gap between what they're interested in and what they're ready for, that's a sign to find a way to build the foundation first, not to skip ahead and hope for the best.

Talk to the school counselor before course selection happens, not after. Schedule a meeting specifically to discuss your child's academic trajectory and ask the counselor directly: based on what you've seen from my child so far, which courses do you think are the right level of challenge for next year? Counselors have seen hundreds of students make these decisions. Their read on your child's readiness is worth more than any ranking of which classes "look best" on an application.

This is where GPA strategy becomes important. For all students considering applying to colleges in the future, GPA is important and protecting it matters. A student who finishes 10th grade with a 3.6 GPA earned in a reasonable mix of standard and honors courses is in a better position than a student who finishes with a 3.1 earned in a schedule packed with AP classes they weren't ready for. The 3.6 student has options. The 3.1 student has a harder story to tell, even if the harder schedule seems more impressive on the surface. Colleges weigh both, but they do so in context, and the context of a low GPA in an overloaded schedule often reads as a student who made a poor decision, not a student who was impressively ambitious.

If your child is already in advanced classes and struggling, the answer isn't always to drop down. Sometimes the answer is targeted support, a tutor for one specific subject, a study group, more consistent use of teacher office hours. But sometimes dropping to a lower level is frankly the right call, and it's worth saying clearly that doing so is not a failure. A student who recognizes they're in over their head, makes a strategic adjustment, and then finishes the year with strong grades in a better-matched course is demonstrating exactly the kind of self-awareness and decision-making that serves people well in college and in life. That's a story worth telling, not hiding.

The goal of 10th grade academics is to build a record that shows consistent effort, appropriate challenge, and genuine competence.

The PSAT, Standardized Testing, and What to Actually Do About It

Most students take the PSAT in October, though some schools also offer the PSAT 10 in the spring. Typically parents receive the score report, look at it briefly, and put it in a drawer without knowing what to do with it. That's a missed opportunity, because the PSAT in 10th grade is actually one of the most useful pieces of information you'll get in this entire process, if you know how to read it.

The PSAT is not the SAT. Your child's score on the 10th grade PSAT does not go to colleges. It doesn't affect their application in any direct way. What it does is give you an early, honest look at where your child stands relative to the skills the SAT tests, reading comprehension, evidence-based writing, and math, before any of it counts. As of April 2026, the PSAT is scored in two sections: Reading & Writing and Math, with scores ranging from 320 to 1520. The two versions, PSAT in the fall and the PSAT 10 in spring (if your school offers it) give your child a chance to see what their strengths are. That's truly valuable. It's like a diagnostic scan before you start treatment. You're not getting results that matter yet. You're getting information that helps you plan.

When the score report comes back, here's how to read it without panicking. The report will show a total score and two section scores: one for Evidence-Based Reading and Writing, and one for Math. It will also show your child's percentile, meaning what percentage of test-takers scored at or below their level. And it will show something called "subscores" that break down performance into more specific skill areas, things like "command of evidence" or "problem-solving and data analysis." These subscores are where the real information lives.

Don't fixate on the total score number. Instead, look at the subscores and find the two or three areas where your child scored lowest relative to the others. Those are the skill gaps. Write them down. Those specific areas are where any future test prep should focus, not broad, general SAT practice, but targeted work on the actual skills that showed up as weak in the diagnostic. That's the difference between efficient preparation and expensive, time-consuming preparation that doesn't move the needle much.

Now, a word about the National Merit Scholarship Program, because it comes up every year and causes confusion. The PSAT taken in 11th grade, not 10th grade, is the qualifying exam for National Merit. Scoring in the top percentile in your state in 11th grade can open doors to scholarships and recognition. The 10th grade PSAT doesn't count for National Merit. But it does give you a full year to work on the specific skills that determine whether your child is competitive in 11th grade. Think of the 10th grade PSAT as the practice round for the practice round. Used well, it's a true advantage.

Here's a practical testing plan you can build right now based on your child's 10th grade PSAT results. First, identify the two weakest subscores. Second, find free or low-cost resources to work on those specific skills. Khan Academy has a free, official SAT prep program that is very good and is tied directly to College Board data. It's not a placeholder for something better. It's actually one of the most effective tools available, and it costs nothing. Have your child spend 20 to 30 minutes, two or three times a week, working on the specific skill areas that showed up as gaps. Not the whole test. Just those areas. Third, plan for your child to take the PSAT again in 11th grade with those gaps reduced. Fourth, based on how the 11th grade PSAT goes, decide whether to take the SAT, the ACT, or both, and when.

The testing question that most parents get wrong is this: should my child take the SAT or the ACT? The honest answer is that some students genuinely do better on one than the other, and you won't know which until your child takes a practice version of both. The SAT and ACT test similar skills but in different formats and with different timing. The ACT has an optional science section that the SAT doesn't. Some students find the ACT's pacing more manageable. Others prefer the SAT's structure. Download a free official practice test for each and have your child take both under timed conditions. Compare the results. Whichever one produces the stronger performance relative to the school ranges your child is targeting is the one to focus on.

One more thing about testing that's worth saying plainly. If your child is applying to test-optional schools and their scores are not competitive for the schools on their list, they don't have to submit them. Test-optional means exactly that. But "test-optional" doesn't mean "test-irrelevant." A strong score at a test-optional school can still strengthen an application. A weak score submitted to a school where the middle 50% of admitted students scored significantly higher creates doubt. Know the ranges. Make a strategic decision. Don't submit scores reflexively, and don't withhold them reflexively either.

Building Real-World Skills Through Everyday Opportunities

There's a skill gap that almost no college prep book talks about, and it's one of the most important ones. It's not a test score gap or a GPA gap. It's the gap between what a student knows how to do on paper and what they're actually capable of doing in the real world when someone is counting on them.

Communication. Problem-solving. Follow-through. The ability to handle something going wrong without falling apart. These are the skills that determine whether your child thrives in college, gets hired after college, keeps the job, gets promoted, builds relationships, and handles adult life with any degree of confidence. And they are not built in a classroom. They're built in the messy, unglamorous, ordinary experiences of everyday life.

The good news is that your child's sophomore year is full of those experiences. The challenge is learning to see them for what they are.

A part-time job, even a few hours a week at a coffee shop or a grocery store or a local restaurant, is one of the most underrated skill-building opportunities available to a high schooler. A student who holds a part-time job learns to show up on time even when they don't feel like it, to take direction from someone who isn't their parent or their teacher, to handle a frustrated customer without taking it personally, and to manage their own time across school and work without someone scheduling it for them. Those are not small things. Those are exactly the skills that employers say most new college graduates are missing. If your child has the opportunity to work part-time without it damaging their academic performance, that experience is worth more than most resume items they could add.

Family responsibilities count too, and this is worth saying clearly for working-class and immigrant families where teenagers often carry actual weight at home. A student who translates for their parents at medical appointments, who cooks dinner while a parent works a second shift, who helps manage a younger sibling's schedule, who handles household logistics because the adults in the family are stretched thin, that student is building real-world skills every single day. The mistake is assuming that these experiences don't count because they're not official or organized. They absolutely count. The challenge is learning to articulate them in a way that makes their value visible.

When it comes time to write college essays, a student who helped run a household, who navigated adult systems on behalf of their family, who took on responsibility most of their peers never had to think about, has genuinely powerful material. But only if they can talk about what they learned from it, not just what they did. The "what I did" part is the surface. The "what I learned" part is the essay. Help your child practice making that connection now, long before they're sitting in front of a blank essay prompt.

Here's a simple habit to build this year. At the end of each week, spend five minutes with your child asking one question: "What's something that was hard this week, and how did you handle it?" It doesn't have to be a big thing. A conflict with a friend. A moment when they had to make a decision on their own. A situation at work or at school where something didn't go as planned. The goal is to get your child in the habit of noticing their own experiences and reflecting on what those experiences taught them. That habit, practiced consistently over the course of a year, produces a teenager who can walk into a college essay or a job interview and talk about themselves with genuine depth and self-awareness. That's not just a soft skill. That's a competitive advantage.

Passion projects deserve a mention here too. A passion project is simply something your child builds or pursues on their own time because they actually want to, not because it was assigned or required. It could be a small YouTube channel about something they're obsessed with. A blog. A community garden. A fundraiser for something they care about. A piece of software they're teaching themselves to build. An independent study in a subject their school doesn't offer. The format doesn't matter much. What matters is that it's self-initiated and self-sustained, because those two qualities are exactly what colleges are looking for and exactly what employers value in new hires.

If your child doesn't have a passion project yet, don't manufacture one. Go back to the thread-finding exercise from the first section of this chapter. The thread points toward the project. A student who's genuinely interested in environmental issues might start tracking local water quality data. A student who loves fashion might start documenting the history of a specific style on a simple blog. A student who's interested in mental health might start a peer support group at their school. None of these require money or connections. They require initiative, that's the deeper value.

The skill-building that happens in 10th grade through jobs, family responsibilities, and passion projects doesn't just produce better college applications. It produces a kid who knows they can figure things out when things get hard. That confidence, earned through tangible experience rather than told to them by a parent, is one of the most valuable things your child can take into their adult life.

What We Covered and Your Action Steps

Sophomore year is the year most families underuse. This chapter was about changing that, giving you a clear picture of what 10th grade is actually for and what to do with it before it's gone.

Finding the thread is the foundation of everything else. A child who knows what they genuinely care about makes better course choices, builds more meaningful activities, writes stronger essays, and walks into the rest of high school with a sense of direction instead of a sense of pressure. The thread-finding exercise in this chapter is the place to start, and it costs nothing but a conversation and 30 minutes of honest attention.

Academic choices in 10th grade set the tone for the second half of high school. The goal is appropriate challenge, not maximum difficulty. A student who earns strong grades in well-matched courses is in a better position than one who earns mediocre grades in courses they weren't ready for. Talk to your child's counselor. Look at the transcript honestly. Make course decisions based on your child's actual readiness, not on what sounds most impressive.

Remember, the PSAT is a tool, not a verdict. Use the score report to identify specific skill gaps, then build a targeted, low-cost plan to address them over the next year. Khan Academy is free and it works. Use it.

Real-world skills are being built right now, in your child's everyday life, whether you're paying attention to them or not. Your job is to make those experiences visible, to help your child reflect on what they're learning, and to frame ordinary responsibility as genuine preparation for what comes next.

Here are your four action steps for this month, in order.

This week, do the thread-finding exercise with your child. Set aside 30 minutes, ask the four questions, write down the answers without commenting, and then ask which one they'd want to explore more. Help them find one concrete next step, one specific opportunity to go deeper into that thing before the school year ends.

Before course selection happens, schedule a meeting with your child's school counselor. Bring your child's current transcript. Ask the counselor directly which courses they think are the right level of challenge for next year based on what they've seen. Then sit down with your child and make the final decision together, based on both their interest and their readiness.

When the PSAT score report arrives, pull out the subscores and identify the two weakest areas. Set up a free Khan Academy account linked to your child's College Board account. Have your child spend 20 to 30 minutes, two or three times a week, working specifically on those skill areas. Put it on the weekly calendar the same way you'd schedule any other commitment.

Start the weekly reflection habit. Every Sunday evening, ask your child one question: "What was something hard this week, and how did you handle it?" Keep it casual. Don't turn it into a debrief. Just get them used to noticing their own experiences and thinking about what those experiences taught them. Do this every week for the rest of the school year. By the time essay season arrives in 11th grade, your child will have a year's worth of authentic material to draw from, and more importantly, they'll already know how to talk about themselves with clarity and honesty.

None of these steps require a counselor, a test prep company, or anything money can't easily cover. They require your attention, your consistency, and your willingness to treat sophomore year as the meaningful year it actually is. The families who do this work in 10th grade don't just end up with stronger applications. They end up with teenagers who know themselves, who've built real skills, and who are genuinely ready for what comes next.

Chapter 4
11th Grade – The Year Everything Counts

Why Junior Year Is the Most Important Year for College Admissions

If you've been paying attention since 9th grade, junior year is where that work starts to pay off. If you're just now waking up to the process, junior year is where you make up ground fast. Either way, 11th grade is the year that carries more weight in a college application than any other, and most families don't fully understand why until they're already deep into it.

Here's the reality. When an admissions officer opens your child's file, the first thing they look at is the academic record. And the year that gets the most scrutiny on that record is 11th grade. Not because 9th and 10th grade don't matter, they do, as we covered in the last two chapters. But junior year is the most recent full year of performance an admissions officer can see when your child applies. It's the clearest signal of who your child is right now, not who they were three years ago. It shows whether the upward trend held, whether the challenge level increased appropriately, and whether the student can sustain strong performance under real pressure. That combination tells a college a lot about what a student will look like in their freshman year.

Junior year is also when most of the standardized testing happens. It's when teacher relationships that lead to recommendation letters need to be actively built. It's when the extracurricular story needs to be deepening rather than widening. And it's when the college essay process, done right, should begin in some form, even if the final drafts don't get written until summer or senior fall.

That's a lot happening at once.

The parents who handle junior year well aren't the ones who panic and try to cram everything in. They're the ones who understand what each piece of the year is actually for and sequence their attention accordingly. The sections in this chapter will give you that sequence, one piece at a time, so the year feels like a plan rather than a sprint toward an invisible finish line.

Another thing that you need to know before we go any further. Junior year is truthfully hard for most teenagers, not just academically, but emotionally. The pressure is real. The stakes feel enormous. And your child is navigating all of it while also being a 16 or 17-year-old who is still figuring out who they are. The way you show up as a parent this year, whether you add to the pressure or help absorb it, will shape not just the college process but your relationship with your teenager for years to come. We'll come back to that at the end of this chapter, because it matters just as much as everything else.

For now, start here. Pull up your child's current transcript and look at the courses they're taking this year. Are they taking the most challenging courses their school offers in the subjects where they're strongest? If not, it's worth a conversation with the school counselor about whether any adjustments are still possible. Admissions officers look specifically at whether a student pushed themselves in 11th grade. A student who coasted through junior year in easy classes sends a signal that no amount of strong essay writing can fully override.

The SAT/ACT Strategy — Testing Smart, Not Just Testing More

Every year, thousands of families make the same testing mistake. Their child takes the SAT or ACT once, gets a score they're not happy with, signs up for every available test date over the next six months, and takes the test again and again with no meaningful change in preparation between attempts. The score barely moves. The stress accumulates. The money disappears. And by the time senior year starts, the family is exhausted from a testing process that never had a real strategy behind it.

Testing more is not the same as testing smarter.

The first decision to make in junior year is whether your child should focus on the SAT or the ACT. If you followed the advice in Chapter 3 and had your child take a timed practice version of both, you already have data to work with. If you haven't done that yet, do it now before anything else. Download a free official SAT practice test from the College Board website and a free official ACT practice test from the ACT website. Have your child take both under real timed conditions, meaning no breaks between sections, no phone, no distractions. Score both tests. Then compare the results not just in raw numbers, but in terms of how close each score is to the ranges of the schools your child is targeting.

The test where your child's practice score is already closer to their target range is the one to focus on. That's it. There's no universally better test. There's only the test that fits how your specific child thinks and works under pressure.

Once you've chosen a test, build a prep plan that's specific and time-limited. What does that mean? Here's what that looks like in practice. Your child takes the chosen test for the first time in the fall of junior year, ideally October or November. Before that test date, they spend six to eight weeks doing targeted preparation, not generic review of everything, but focused work on the specific skill areas that showed up as weakest on their practice test. Khan Academy's free SAT prep is very effective and directly tied to College Board data. For the ACT, the official ACT prep materials and PrepScholar's free resources are solid starting points. The preparation should be consistent, meaning 30 to 45 minutes, four or five days a week, rather than sporadic marathon sessions the week before the test.

After the first real test, look at the score report carefully. Every official score report breaks down performance by skill area, just like the PSAT report we discussed in Chapter 3. Find the two or three areas where your child lost the most points. Those are the only areas that need focused attention before the next attempt. Then schedule one more test date, typically in the winter or early spring of junior year, and repeat the targeted prep process for those specific areas only.

Two well-prepared attempts is almost always more effective than four or five attempts with no real change in preparation. Most students see their biggest score gains between their first and second attempt, when they have real test experience to draw from and specific weaknesses to address. After the second attempt, the gains tend to diminish unless there's been significant additional learning, not just more practice tests.

Now, about test-optional policies. Many schools went test-optional during the pandemic and have kept that policy. But test-optional doesn't mean test-irrelevant, and it doesn't mean the same thing at every school. At some schools, submitting a strong score strengthens an application. At others, the essay and extracurricular record carry far more weight than any test score. The only way to know which category a school falls into is to look at their specific data. Check whether the school publishes information about what percentage of admitted students submitted scores and what the score ranges were for those who did. If the school shows that nearly all admitted students submitted scores and the ranges are high, a strong score matters there. If the data shows a wide mix, the school is really treating the test as optional.

For families where test prep costs are a real concern, here's what's available at no cost. College Board's official SAT practice on Khan Academy is free and personalized. Many public libraries offer free access to test prep resources and sometimes free prep classes. Fee waivers for the SAT and ACT are available to students who qualify based on family income, and your child's school counselor can provide those waivers. Don't let cost be the reason your child doesn't prepare. The free resources, used consistently, are genuinely effective.

One final word on testing. If your child has a documented learning difference or disability, they may qualify for extended time or other accommodations on standardized tests. This process takes time to set up, sometimes several months, and requires documentation from a qualified professional. If this applies to your child, start that process now, not the week before the test. Talk to your child's school counselor or a specialist about what documentation is needed and how to apply for accommodations through College Board or ACT. Your child deserves to be tested under conditions that give them a fair shot.

Building a Relationship With Teachers for Powerful Recommendation Letters

Most students think about recommendation letters for the first time in September of senior year, when the application deadlines are already visible on the calendar and the panic has set in. They approach a teacher they've had for one semester, ask for a letter with a few weeks' notice, and receive something politely generic that confirms the student showed up and did the work. That letter doesn't hurt the application, but it doesn't help it either.

The students who get the letters that actually move an admissions decision are the ones who spent junior year building real relationships with two or three teachers, without ever once mentioning the word "recommendation."

That's the key. You don't build a relationship with a teacher in order to get a letter. You build a real relationship, and the letter is the natural result of that relationship. Admissions officers read thousands of recommendation letters every cycle. They can tell immediately whether a teacher honestly knows and cares about a student or is filling out a form. The letters that stand out are specific. They reference actual moments, actual conversations, actual growth. They tell a story about a real person that the grades and test scores can't tell on their own. The only way a teacher can write that kind of letter is if they honestly know your child that well.

Here's how to help your child build those relationships deliberately but authentically during junior year. Start by identifying the right teachers. The best recommenders are not necessarily the teachers your child got the highest grades from. They're the teachers your child has had a real interaction with, the ones who have seen your child struggle and push through, who have had a conversation with your child outside of class, who teach a subject that connects to your child's genuine interests or intended direction. Two strong recommendations from teachers who truly know your child are worth far more than three polished letters from teachers who barely remember their name.

Once your child has identified one or two teachers they'd like to build a stronger relationship with, the next step is simple: show up. If the teacher offers office hours during their planning period, show up, not just when there's a test coming up, but to ask a real question about something in the material. Contribute to class discussions in a way that shows real thinking, not just the right answer. After a class where something was particularly interesting, say so. Not in a flattering way, but in a real way: "That discussion about X made me think about Y. Can I ask you something about that?" These moments, accumulated over months, are what a teacher draws on when they sit down to write a letter.

Your child should also share things with these teachers that connect their classwork to their real life. If a student in an English class is working on a personal writing project outside of school, mentioning that to the teacher creates a fuller picture of who they are. If a student in a history class is truly curious about a connection between what they're studying and something happening in the world right now, that conversation sticks with a teacher in a way that a strong essay grade alone doesn't.

When it's time to actually ask for the letter, the timing and the ask itself matter. The right time to ask is in the spring of junior year, not the fall of senior year. Asking in the spring gives teachers the entire summer to think about what they want to write and to do it without the pressure of twenty other seniors asking at the same time. Whenever possible, your child should speak to the teacher in person, even if the formal request is also sent by email. That brief conversation helps the teacher connect a face and personality to the request and makes it less likely the email gets lost in a crowded inbox. Your email should sound something like this: "I've really valued being in your class this year, and I feel like you've seen me grow in ways that matter to me. I'm going to be applying to college in the fall, and I was hoping you'd be willing to write a recommendation letter for me. I completely understand if you're not able to, and I wanted to give you as much time as possible."

That phrasing does three things. It expresses genuine appreciation. It gives the teacher an easy out if they're not comfortable, which actually increases the chance they'll say yes because they don't feel trapped. And it gives them time, which every teacher appreciates.

After the teacher agrees, your child should follow-up with an email confirming the conversation and give them a one-page document called a "brag sheet" or a "student information sheet." I know some teachers who even create their own for students to fill out. Some even have parents fill out a sheet about their child too. This is not a resume. It's a personal document that gives the teacher material to work with. It should include two or three specific moments or interactions your child remembers from their class, what your child feels they learned or how they grew in that class, what your child is most proud of from their time in school so far, and what they hope to do after high school. This document makes the teacher's job easier and makes the resulting letter more specific and more powerful. Most students never provide anything like this, which is exactly why most recommendation letters are generic.

For immigrant families or families where the culture doesn't typically encourage children to "promote" themselves to authority figures, this process can feel uncomfortable. It can feel like bragging, or like being too forward. It's worth reframing it this way: your child isn't asking for a favor. They're giving a teacher the opportunity to advocate for a student they genuinely care about. Teachers who write strong letters almost always feel good about doing it. They want their students to succeed. Your child is making it possible for that to happen by building a real relationship and making the ask in a respectful, timely way.

Starting the College Essay — Earlier Than You Think

The college essay is the part of the application that most parents understand the least and most students dread the most. And the biggest mistake families make with it, by a wide margin, is starting too late.

Most students begin thinking seriously about their college essay in August before senior year. Some start in September. A few start in October, which is already dangerously close to Early Decision and Early Action deadlines. By that point, the essay is being written under enormous pressure, with a tight deadline, on top of senior year coursework, and alongside the rest of the application. The result is almost always an essay that's rushed, generic, or both.

The students who write memorable essays almost always started the brainstorming process in junior year.

That doesn't mean they wrote a finished essay in 11th grade. It means they spent time during junior year doing something far more valuable than writing: figuring out what they actually want to say. The brainstorming process, finding the story worth telling, is the hardest part of the college essay. The writing itself, once you know what you're writing about, is much more manageable. Starting the thinking in junior year means your child arrives at the summer before senior year with a clear direction and a head start, instead of a blank page and a deadline.

Here's what the college essay is actually for, because most families misunderstand this. The essay is not a summary of your child's accomplishments. It's not a chance to list everything they've done and explain why they deserve to be admitted. It's not a formal piece of writing that shows off vocabulary. It's a window into who your child is as a person, how they think, what they notice, what they care about, and how they make sense of their own experience. The best essays are often about something that seems small on the surface but reveals something large and true about the person writing it.

Think about the difference between an essay about winning a state championship and an essay about the moment before a big game when your child realized they were more nervous about letting down their teammate than about losing. The first essay is about an achievement. The second essay is about a person. Admissions officers have read ten thousand essays about achievements. They remember the essays about people.

To help your child start this process in junior year, use these three prompts as starting points for a conversation. You can reword them to match the way you actually speak. After all, we want them to answer honestly and naturally. Don't present them as homework or all at once. Just ask them casually, maybe in the car or over dinner, and see what comes up.

First prompt: "What's something you've changed your mind about in the last two or three years, and what changed it?" Second prompt: "When have you felt most like yourself, doing what, and why do you think that is?" Third prompt: "What's something about your life or your background that most people at your school don't know, and that you think actually shaped who you are?"

These questions don't have right answers. They're designed to surface the kind of material that makes for a genuine essay, specific, personal, and rooted in real experience. Whatever your child says in response to these questions, even if it's just a fragment of an idea, write it down. You're building a bank of raw material that the essay will eventually come from.

For families where English is not the first language at home, the college essay can feel especially intimidating. Parents may worry that their child's writing won't sound sophisticated enough, or that their story won't seem impressive compared to students from more privileged backgrounds. This is worth addressing directly. Admissions officers are not looking for the most eloquent prose. They're looking for the most authentic voice. A student who writes in a clear, honest, specific way about a real experience will always outperform a student who writes in a polished but hollow way about something they think sounds impressive. Your child's background, their experience navigating between cultures, their role in their family, the things they've had to figure out that their peers never had to think about, that is not a disadvantage in the college essay. It's material. Rich, specific, real material that most applicants don't have access to.

One practical step to take this month: have your child write one paragraph, just one, about a moment from the last year that they remember clearly and that meant something to them. It doesn't have to be dramatic. It doesn't have to be polished. It just has to be honest and specific. Put it in a document and save it. Do this once a month for the rest of junior year.

By the time summer arrives, your child will have a collection of moments and ideas to draw from, and the essay will start to write itself.

Managing Stress Without Losing the Relationship

Junior year stress is real. It's not something your teenager is making up or exaggerating. The pressure of harder classes, standardized testing, extracurricular commitments, and the growing awareness that college applications are coming, all of it lands at once during a developmental stage when teenagers are already carrying more emotional weight than most adults remember. The stress is real, and how you respond to it will either make this year easier for your child or significantly harder.

The most common mistake parents make during junior year is adding to the pressure while believing they're reducing it. It sounds like: "You need to study more for the SAT." "Did you talk to your teacher about that grade?" "Other kids are already thinking about their college lists, are you?" These statements come from love and from genuine fear. But what a stressed teenager hears is: you're not doing enough, I'm worried about you, and you're falling behind. That message, repeated enough times, doesn't motivate. It shuts people down.

Your child doesn't need you to remind them that junior year matters. They already know. What they need is someone who can be calm when everything else feels chaotic.

There's a real difference between being overwhelmed and being uncomfortable, and learning to tell the difference as a parent is one of the most important skills you can develop this year. Uncomfortable is normal. A teenager who's stressed about an upcoming AP exam, who's tired from a long week, who's anxious about a test score, is experiencing the ordinary difficulty of a hard year. That discomfort is not a sign that something is wrong. It's a sign that they're doing something challenging, which is exactly what they should be doing. Your job in those moments is to acknowledge the difficulty without trying to immediately fix it. "That sounds really hard. What do you need right now?" is more useful than "Here's what you should do."

Overwhelmed is different. Overwhelmed looks like a teenager who has stopped sleeping consistently, who has withdrawn from things they used to enjoy, who seems unable to function in daily life, who talks about feeling hopeless or like nothing they do matters. These are signs that the stress has crossed a line that needs real attention, not just encouragement. If you're seeing these signs in your child, the right response is not to push through and hope they find their footing. It's to slow down, talk to them directly, and if needed, connect them with a school counselor or a therapist who can provide real support. Academic performance matters, but your child's mental health is not something to sacrifice for a college application.

Consider a hypothetical parent named Diane. She is 45 years old and works as an office manager. Her 16-year-old son Marcus is in the middle of junior year. Marcus is a solid student, mostly As and Bs, and he's been working hard. But Diane has been reading about college admissions, talking to other parents, and she's convinced he's not doing enough. She starts bringing up the SAT at dinner. She emails his counselor without telling him. She texts him during the school day to ask if he's studied. Marcus stops talking to her about school entirely. By February, he's not sharing anything with her, not his test scores, not his stress, not his worries. She's the last person he'd go to if something went wrong. Diane's fear was real and her love was genuine, but the way she expressed it pushed her son away at exactly the moment he needed her most.

This pattern shows up in families everywhere, across every background and income level. The relationship is the most powerful tool you have this year. A teenager who trusts their parent, who feels safe being honest about what's hard, who knows they won't be judged or immediately lectured is a teenager who can handle more pressure. Because they're not carrying it alone.

Here are specific things you can do to protect that relationship during junior year. First, create one regular moment each week that has nothing to do with school or college. A walk. A show you watch together. A meal where the rule is no college talk. This isn't avoidance. It's maintenance. It keeps the relationship from becoming entirely defined by the stress of the process.

Second, ask your child directly and regularly: "What do you need from me right now?" Then listen to the answer. Sometimes they'll say they need help. Sometimes they'll say they need you to back off. Both answers are useful. Taking that answer seriously, even when it's hard to hear, builds the kind of trust that makes the harder conversations possible later.

Third, watch your own anxiety. Your fear about your child's future is real, and it's understandable. But your teenager is not responsible for managing your anxiety. When you feel the urge to check their grades for the third time this week, or to bring up the SAT when you promised yourself you wouldn't, recognize that urge for what it is and find somewhere else to put it. Talk to a friend. Write it down. Call your spouse or partner. Your child needs you regulated, not perfect, just regulated enough to be a steady presence in a year that doesn't feel steady.

The parents who come out of junior year with a strong relationship with their teenager are not the ones who did everything right. They're the ones who kept showing up, kept listening, and kept choosing the relationship over the impulse to control the outcome. That choice, made again and again across the course of a year, is what your child will remember long after the acceptance letters are forgotten.

Your Junior Year Game Plan — Semester by Semester

Junior year is long enough to feel manageable if you break it into two distinct phases. The fall semester and the spring semester each have their own priorities, and knowing which to focus on when takes the guesswork out of the year.

In the fall semester, your attention goes to four things. Academics come first, specifically making sure your child is taking the right level of courses and getting the support they need early, before small struggles become big grade problems. The first standardized test attempt belongs in the fall, ideally October or November, after six to eight weeks of targeted preparation. Teacher relationships should be actively built this semester, not saved for spring. And the college essay brainstorming should begin, using the prompts from the earlier section in this chapter, in a low-pressure way that doesn't feel like an assignment.

In the spring semester, the focus shifts. A second test attempt, if needed, should happen in February, March, or April, with targeted prep between attempts. The college list should start taking shape, not a final list, but a working list of schools your child is honestly interested in, organized by reach, match, and safety. Your child should ask for recommendation letters in April or May, in person, with enough advance notice to give teachers the entire summer. And the essay direction, not the finished essay, but the story your child wants to tell, should be clear by the end of junior year.

Here are your specific action steps, organized so you know exactly what to do and when.

This month, if you haven't already, have your child take a timed practice version of both the SAT and the ACT. Score both. Choose the test where their practice score is already closer to their target school ranges. Register for a fall test date. Set up a prep schedule of 30 to 45 minutes, four to five days a week, focused on the specific skill areas that showed up weakest on the practice test.

Before winter break, sit down with your child and ask the three essay brainstorming prompts from the earlier section. Don't pressure them to have answers immediately. Let the questions sit. Have them write one paragraph about one specific moment from the last year and save it. Do this once a month for the rest of the year.

In January or February, look at your child's current grades in every class. If anything is below a B, schedule a conversation with the teacher now, not at the end of the semester. Ask what support is available and help your child take the first step in reaching out themselves.

In April, help your child identify two teachers to ask for recommendation letters. Coach them on how to make the ask in person. Help them prepare a one-page brag sheet to give each teacher after the ask. Make sure the ask happens before the school year ends.

By the end of May, have a working college list of ten to fifteen schools with each one labeled as reach, match, or safety. For each school, look up the current acceptance rate, the middle 50% GPA and test score range, and the net price calculator result for your family's income level. This research takes a few hours and changes every decision that comes after it.

Junior year is the year where the foundation built in 9th and 10th grade either shows up or doesn't. The habits your child built around managing their time, advocating for themselves, and recovering from setbacks are going to be tested this year in real ways. Your job isn't to protect them from that pressure. It's to make sure they don't face it alone. The kid who gets through junior year with their confidence intact, with a real relationship with their parent, and with a clear sense of what they want to say about themselves, that kid doesn't just have a strong college application. They have something that lasts a lot longer than that.

Chapter 5
12th Grade — Executing the Plan and Letting Go

Senior year arrives and something shifts in the air of your house. You can feel it. Your child is almost gone, not in a bad way, but in the way you always hoped for when you were up at 2am with a sick toddler or sitting in a school parking lot waiting for them to come out. This is what all of it was building toward. And now that it's here, it feels like there's more to do than ever and less time to do it.

That feeling is partly right. Senior year is genuinely busy. But it's also manageable if you know what you're trying to accomplish and what you can let go of. Most families treat 12th grade like a sprint when it's really a series of very specific, very sequential moves. The families who get through it with their sanity and their relationships intact are the ones who had a clear picture of what mattered and when.

This chapter gives you that picture.

Senior Year Priorities — What Actually Matters Now

Senior year has a way of feeling urgent about everything at once. Applications. Deadlines. Grades. Senior activities. Financial aid forms. It all lands in the same few months and it can feel like you're constantly behind no matter how much you do. The families who navigate this well aren't the ones doing the most. They're the ones doing the right things in the right order.

So let's be direct about what actually matters in 12th grade and what doesn't.

Grades still matter. This is the part most students don't fully believe, and some parents don't push back on hard enough. There's a widespread assumption that once applications are submitted, grades become irrelevant. They don't. Colleges send acceptance letters with a condition attached, even if it's not stated explicitly: maintain your academic performance. Every year, colleges rescind acceptances from students whose senior year grades dropped significantly. It's not common, but it happens, and it happens to students who truly believed they were done once they hit submit. Beyond rescission, your child's first-semester senior grades may be requested by schools that defer them from Early Action or Early Decision rounds. A strong first semester can tip a deferred application toward acceptance. A weak one confirms doubt.

The practical target is this: your child should aim to finish the first semester of senior year with grades as close to their junior year performance as possible. Not identical, necessarily, but close. A slight dip is normal and generally understood. A dramatic drop is a problem.

What doesn't matter as much as most parents think? Adding new activities in senior year to bulk up the application. Admissions officers can tell when a student joined a club in September of 12th grade specifically to list it on their application. It doesn't add anything. If your child isn't already involved in something meaningful, the answer isn't to manufacture involvement at the last minute. It's to write honestly about what they have been doing and why it matters. Substance always beats padding.

The application deadlines themselves deserve a calendar of their own. If you haven't already built one, do it today. Write down every school on your child's list, the application type, the deadline date, and the financial aid deadline, because those are often different and missing the financial aid deadline can cost your family real money regardless of whether your child gets accepted. A shared Google calendar that both you and your child can see works well. Color-code by urgency if that helps. The goal is that no deadline ever sneaks up on you because you weren't tracking it.

Motivation is the other thing that needs active management in senior year. There's a well-documented phenomenon called "senioritis" that hits most 12th graders at some point, usually after applications are submitted. The sense of purpose that kept them going evaporates, and school starts to feel pointless when the finish line is already in sight. This is real, and it's not a character flaw. But it needs to be managed.

The best way to help your child stay motivated isn't to lecture them about grades. It's to keep the connection between their daily effort and their actual future visible. When they're tempted to coast, remind them specifically what's at stake, not in a scary way, but in a real one. "Your first semester grades could matter if you get deferred. Let's keep the option open." That's a concrete reason, not a vague threat. Concrete reasons work better with teenagers than abstract ones.

Managing multiple application deadlines without a meltdown comes down to one thing: starting earlier than feels necessary. Most students underestimate how long applications really take to complete properly. The Common App itself is relatively fast to fill out. But the essays take multiple drafts. The activity descriptions require careful thought and precise word choices within a limited character count. Not every Admissions reader may know that "GSA" stands for Gay-Straight Alliance at your school and not General Services Administration. If there is any doubt, spell it out.

Requesting official transcripts takes time. Most colleges and universities accept these from your school electronically. So make sure your student requests them through Common App or the application (if it's a stand-alone). Don't make their counseling office print out official transcripts to mail in if they aren't needed. Sending test scores officially takes time. Letters of recommendation need to be submitted by the teacher, and teachers have their own timelines. Every piece of the application has a longer lead time than it appears, and when you're managing five, ten, or fifteen schools at once, those lead times stack up fast.

Here's the specific timeline that works. For any Early Decision or Early Action deadline in November, every piece of the application should be complete and ready to submit by October 15th at the latest. That includes finalized essays, the activity section, all test scores sent, and confirmation that recommenders have submitted their letters. The two-week buffer before the actual deadline is not optional padding. It's protection against the technical issues, the forgotten password, the transcript that didn't send, the recommender who needed a reminder, all of which happen to someone every single year.

And you should be aware that some state schools, ones that draw a lot of applications from out of state students, have single regular decision deadlines that are much earlier than January. (Georgia Tech, I'm looking at you). So if your child is applying to your state flagship university make sure they double check the deadline and adjust their timeline accordingly.

For Regular Decision deadlines in January, every piece should be complete by December 15th. Your child should not be writing essays on December 31st. Not because it's impossible, but because the essays written under that kind of pressure are almost never as good as the ones written with time to breathe and revise. And during winter break, school staff may not be available to help resolve missing transcript or recommendation issues.

One more aspect of senior year priorities that often gets overlooked - and this is important. Your child needs to take care of themselves this year. Sleep. Food. Time with friends that has nothing to do with college. These aren't luxuries. A teenager who is running on fumes, skipping meals, and sacrificing every social connection for the sake of applications is not producing their best work. They're producing stressed, exhausted work. The students who submit the strongest applications are almost always the ones who stayed reasonably rested and connected to their life outside of the process. That balance is worth protecting, even when the calendar makes it feel impossible. Their mental health matters.

Writing and Submitting a Standout Application

The application is not a form. A form is something you fill out. An application is something you build. Every piece of it, the essay, the activity descriptions, the short answers, the additional information section, should work together to tell one coherent story about who your child is. When an admissions officer finishes reading the full file, they should feel like they know this person. Not just what they did, but who they are.

That doesn't happen by accident. It happens because someone thought carefully about what story they were telling before they started filling things in.

The college essay is the centerpiece of that story, and if your child followed the advice in Chapter 4 and spent junior year brainstorming, they should already have a direction. If they're starting fresh now, that's okay too, but they need to start immediately. The single most important thing to understand about the college essay is this: the topic matters far less than the execution. A student can write a compelling essay about losing a soccer game. Another student can write a boring essay about surviving cancer. The difference isn't the subject. It's whether the person writing it is actually present on the page, honest, specific, and self-aware.

Here's the process that works for writing a strong college essay, broken into clear steps.

Step one is choosing the right topic. The right topic is not the most impressive thing your child has done. It's the thing they can write about with the most honesty and specificity. Ask your child: what's a moment, experience, or part of your life that you could talk about for an hour without running out of things to say? That's usually where the best essay lives. It might be something small. A conversation they keep thinking about. A habit they developed. A mistake they made and what they did with it. Small and specific almost always beats big and vague. Most of the best essays I've read in the past 20 years have been about something that may feel insignificant to others but had a personal impact on the student: the straight "A" student who forgot where they parked their car and assumed it was stolen; fishing trips with a grandparent; getting lost during a cross country race. What made these so great wasn't the experience itself, but what the student learned from it.

Step two is writing a rough draft with no editing. Tell your child to write the whole thing without stopping to fix sentences or question word choices or worrying about length. The first draft's only job is to exist. It doesn't need to be good. It needs to be done. Most students spend so long trying to write a perfect first sentence that they never get to the part where the real essay is hiding, which is usually somewhere in the middle of the mess.

Step three is reading it out loud. Every single time. When your child reads their essay out loud, they immediately hear the sentences that don't sound like them. The ones that are trying too hard. The ones that sound like they were written for an admissions officer rather than by a real person. Those sentences need to go. The goal is an essay that sounds exactly like your child at their most thoughtful and honest. Not more formal than that. Not more polished than that. Exactly that.

Step four is getting feedback from one or two trusted readers. Not ten people. Not a committee. One parent and one other adult who knows your child well, maybe a teacher or a school counselor. The feedback you're looking for is specific: does this sound like my child? Is there a moment in this essay where you felt like you really understood who they are? Is there anything confusing or anything that feels fake? You're not looking for someone to rewrite the essay. You're looking for a reader's honest reaction.

This brings up the most important boundary in the entire application process, and it's one that parents cross more often than they realize. You cannot write your child's essay. Not a sentence. Not a paragraph. Not a "light edit" that turns their words into yours. Admissions officers read thousands of essays written by 17-year-olds. They know what a 17-year-old sounds like. When an essay sounds like it was written by a 45-year-old with a graduate degree, they notice. And when they notice, the entire application loses credibility, because the one piece that was supposed to show them who this person really is turns out to be someone else's voice. Your job is to ask good questions, give honest reactions, and encourage your child to keep going. The words have to be theirs.

Supplemental essays deserve as much attention as the main essay, and most students give them far less. Supplemental essays are the school-specific short essays that many colleges require in addition to the main Common App essay. The most common one is the "Why us?" essay, where the student explains why they want to attend that specific school. This essay is a test. Admissions officers can immediately tell the difference between a student who did real research and a student who swapped out the school name from a template. A strong "Why us?" essay mentions specific programs, specific professors, specific aspects of the campus culture or curriculum that connect directly to what the student wants to do. Not vague things like "your commitment to excellence" or "the beautiful campus." Specific things that prove the student actually looked.

To write a strong "Why us?" essay, your child should spend at least 30 minutes on the school's website before writing a word. They should look at the specific major or program they're interested in, find two or three professors whose research or teaching connects to their interests, look at student organizations or programs that align with what they care about, and read recent news about the school. Then write the essay using those specifics. It takes more time than a generic essay, but it's the difference between an essay that helps and one that gets forgotten.

Most applicants underuse the activities section, and that's a missed opportunity. Each activity gets a brief description, usually 150 characters or fewer, which is almost nothing. But those 150 characters are a chance to show depth, not just list what your child did. The difference between "Member of robotics club" and "Built and programmed autonomous robot that placed 3rd at regional competition; mentored two younger members" is enormous. One is a label. The other is a story. Every activity description should answer two questions: what did you actually do, and what impact did it have or what did you learn? If your child can't answer both of those questions for an activity, it probably shouldn't be on the list at all.

Before hitting submit on any application, do a final review together. Not to rewrite anything, but to read the whole application as a package and ask one question: does this tell a coherent story about one specific person? If the essay is about leadership and the activities show no evidence of it, there's a disconnect. If the essay is about a passion for science and the activities section has no science-related involvement, that's a gap. The goal is consistency across every piece of the file. Not that everything has to be about the same topic, but that everything points toward the same person-your child. Read it the way an admissions officer would, from the top of the file to the bottom, and ask: do I feel like I know this person? If the answer is yes, it's ready. If the answer is not quite, figure out what's missing and address it before submitting.

One specific thing worth checking before every submission: the name of the school. It sounds absurd, but students submit essays every year with the wrong school's name in them, a leftover from copying and pasting a supplemental essay template. Read every essay one final time with fresh eyes, specifically looking for any reference to a school name, and make sure it matches the school you're submitting to. This is a five-minute check that takes exactly zero skill and can save your child from a genuinely embarrassing mistake.

Handling Rejections, Waitlists, and the Emotional Aftermath

At some point during this process, your child is going to get a rejection. Maybe one. Maybe several. For most families applying to selective schools, rejection is not a possibility. It's a near-certainty for at least one school on the list. And the way your family handles that moment will teach your child something they'll carry for the rest of their life.

That's not an exaggeration. How a person responds to being told no, to being evaluated and found not quite right for something they wanted is one of the most important emotional skills there is. And your child is watching how you respond just as closely as they're managing their own feelings about it.

Before the decisions come out, it's worth having an honest conversation about expectations. Not a pessimistic one, but a realistic one. Selective schools reject the majority of their applicants, including many students who are truly excellent. Being rejected from a school with a 12% acceptance rate doesn't mean your child wasn't good enough. It means 88 out of every 100 applicants weren't admitted, including students with perfect GPAs, perfect test scores, and extraordinary accomplishments. The math alone makes rejection the most common outcome at selective schools. Understanding that before the decisions arrive takes some of the personal sting out of it when it happens.

When a rejection does come, the first thing your child needs is space to feel it. Not a silver lining. Not a lecture about how that school wasn't right for them anyway. Not a reminder that they still have other options. Just acknowledgment. "I know this is disappointing. It's okay to feel that way." That's it. That's the whole first response. Most parents rush past this part because watching their child hurt is unbearable, and fixing it feels like the right thing to do. But a teenager who doesn't get to feel their disappointment doesn't process it. They just carry it around until it comes out sideways somewhere else.

Give it a day. Let the feeling exist. Then, when your child is ready, not when you are, you can have the forward-looking conversation. That conversation isn't about the rejection. It's about the schools that said yes, or that haven't responded yet. It's about what comes next. The question to ask is: "Of the schools you still have options with, which ones are you actually excited about?" That question redirects attention toward possibility without dismissing what just happened. It's a small shift in language that makes a real difference in how the conversation lands.

Waitlists deserve their own honest conversation, because they're genuinely ambiguous and that ambiguity is hard to sit with. Being waitlisted means the school hasn't said no, but they haven't said yes either. For most students, a waitlist is a polite deferral that doesn't result in admission. That's the honest truth, and your child deserves to hear it without cruelty. At the same time, waitlists do move at some schools, and a student who really wants to attend has every right to make their case.

If your child wants to stay on a waitlist, here's the specific process. First, confirm their spot on the waitlist by the deadline the school gives, usually a few weeks after the initial decision. Second, write a letter of continued interest. This letter should be one page, addressed to the admissions office, and should do three things: reaffirm that this school is a genuine first choice and that your child will attend if admitted, share any meaningful updates since the application was submitted, such as a new award, a significant project completed, or a grade that came in stronger than expected, and express specific reasons why this school is the right fit. The letter should be sent by email to the admissions office and should be professional, warm, and brief. Not desperate. Not a list of accomplishments. Just a clear, genuine expression of continued interest with something new to add.

Third, and this is the part most families skip: move forward. Your child should accept an offer from one of their other schools by May 1st, pay the enrollment deposit, and plan accordingly. Staying on a waitlist does not mean putting your life on hold. It means keeping a door open while walking through another one. If the waitlist comes through in June or July, your child can make a new decision at that point. But they cannot spend the spring in limbo, waiting for a school that may never call.

There's a deeper conversation worth having with your child somewhere in the middle of all this, not in the heat of a rejection, but in a calmer moment. It's about what a college acceptance actually means and what it doesn't. An acceptance letter is not a verdict on your child's worth as a person. It's not proof that they're smart, talented, or destined for great things. It's an institutional decision made by a committee working with incomplete information under real constraints, trying to build a specific class for a specific year. The students who thrive in college and in life are not always the ones who got into their first-choice school. They're the ones who showed up, worked hard, and made the most of wherever they landed.

Think about a student, a 17-year-old named James whose parents immigrated from the Philippines and who worked incredibly hard throughout high school. He had a 3.8 GPA, strong test scores, and a real spike in community organizing. He applied to eight schools, including two reaches. Both reaches rejected him. He was devastated. His parents, who had sacrificed enormously, felt it too. But James enrolled at his match school, a solid state university with a strong political science program, and threw himself into it completely. Within two years he was leading a campus organization, had built real relationships with two professors who became mentors, and had secured a competitive internship. The school that rejected him didn't define his outcome. What he did after the rejection did. This scenario reflects something true about how college outcomes actually work in the real world.

For immigrant parents especially, a rejection can feel like a personal failure, like the sacrifice wasn't enough, like the dream fell short. It's worth naming that feeling directly if you're experiencing it, because your child can feel it even when you don't say it out loud. The most powerful thing you can do in that moment is separate your child's worth from the outcome. Not just in what you say, but in how you carry yourself. When your child sees you handle disappointment with grace and forward focus, they learn that skill by watching you. That's not a small thing. That's one of the most important lessons of the whole four-year process.

Rejection is not the end of the story. It's just a chapter that didn't go the way you hoped. The story keeps going, and your child is still the one writing it.

Recap: What We Covered and Your Action Steps

Senior year asks three things of you and your child. Stay focused on what actually matters. Submit a strong, honest, coherent application. And handle whatever comes back with grace, perspective, and a clear sense of what comes next.

None of those three things are easy. But all of them are doable, and all of them build something in your child that lasts far beyond the college decision.

The habits your child has been building since 9th grade, managing their time, advocating for themselves, recovering from setbacks, telling a coherent story about who they are, all of it comes together in senior year. The application is the test of those habits. And how they handle the outcome is the final exam on resilience. A kid who gets through this process with their confidence intact, with a real relationship with their parent, and with a clear sense of what they're moving toward, that kid is ready. Not just for college. For everything after it.

Here are your specific action steps, organized by what to do and when.

This week, build the deadline calendar. Every school on your child's list goes on it, with the application deadline, the financial aid deadline, and the decision type. Share it with your child. Make it something you both own together. Then work backward from each deadline and mark the date by which every piece of that application needs to be complete, two weeks before the actual deadline for Early Decision and Early Action schools, and state schools with early regular admissions dates, and by December 15th for Regular Decision schools.

In the next two weeks, do a full application review together. Read the entire application as a package, from top to bottom. Ask: does this tell a coherent story about one specific person? Check every activity description to make sure it answers both what your child did and what it produced. Read every essay out loud. Check every school-specific essay for the correct school name. Look for any gap between what the essay says about your child and what the rest of the application shows.

Before decisions start arriving, have the expectations conversation. Sit down with your child and talk honestly about the range of possible outcomes. Not to scare them, but to prepare them. Acknowledge that selective schools reject most applicants. Talk about what a rejection means and what it doesn't. Ask your child which schools on their list they'd genuinely be happy attending, beyond just the reaches. Make sure there are real answers to that question before the decisions come in.

When a rejection or waitlist decision arrives, give your child one full day to feel it without trying to fix it. Then, when they're ready, ask the forward-looking question: "Which of your other options are you actually excited about?" If your child wants to pursue a waitlist, help them write a letter of continued interest using the three-part structure from this chapter. And regardless of waitlist status, make sure they accept an offer and pay an enrollment deposit at a school they're actually happy about by May 1st.

Finally, take a moment sometime in the spring, after the decisions are in and the choice is made, to reflect together on the last four years. Not on the outcome, but on the process. Ask your child: what's something you're proud of from high school that has nothing to do with where you got in? Let them answer. Whatever they say, that's the real result of everything you've been building together since 9th grade. The acceptance letter opened a door. The person walking through it is who you were always trying to raise.

Chapter 6
The Money Chapter – Navigating Financial Aid, Scholarships, and Smart College Choices

College costs are one of the most stressful parts of this entire process, and they're also one of the most misunderstood. Most families spend months focused on grades, essays, and applications without ever sitting down to figure out what they can honestly afford. Then the acceptance letters arrive, the financial aid packages come with them, and suddenly the whole conversation shifts from "where does my child want to go" to "how on earth are we going to pay for this."

That sequence is backwards. And it costs families real money.

The families who navigate college finances well aren't necessarily the ones with the most money. They're the ones who understood the financial side of the process early enough to make decisions that protected them. They knew which schools were likely to offer their child significant aid. They filed their paperwork on time. They read the award letters carefully instead of just looking at the bottom line. And they had honest conversations with their teenager about money before the acceptance letters created a situation where those conversations were painful instead of productive.

This chapter covers all of it. Not in a way that requires a finance degree, but in a way that gives you the specific knowledge you need to make genuinely informed decisions. The financial side of college prep is learnable. You don't need a private counselor or a wealthy network to figure this out. You need the right information, and that's what this chapter is for.

Why Financial Fit Is Just as Important as Academic Fit

There's a version of the college decision that plays out in thousands of families every single year, and it almost always ends the same painful way. A student gets into their dream school. Everyone celebrates. The family fills out the financial aid forms, gets the award letter, and discovers that after all the aid and grants and scholarships, they're still looking at $35,000 or $40,000 a year out of pocket. Nobody had run those numbers beforehand. Nobody had talked about what was actually affordable. And now the family is stuck between crushing their child's dream and taking on debt that could follow them for decades.

That situation is preventable. But only if you treat the financial question as seriously as the academic one, starting now, not after the acceptance letters arrive.

Financial fit means choosing schools where the real cost, after all aid is applied, works for your family's actual financial situation. Not the sticker price. Not the advertised tuition. The real number your family would pay out of pocket every year. That number can be wildly different from the sticker price, and it varies enormously from school to school even among schools with similar academic profiles. Two schools with the same tuition rate can leave a family paying $15,000 a year at one and $45,000 a year at the other, depending on how each school calculates and awards financial aid.

Understanding this changes how you build the college list.

A school that offers your child significant merit aid might be a smarter choice than a more prestigious school that offers almost nothing. That's a sentence that makes a lot of parents uncomfortable, because it feels like settling. It isn't. A student who graduates with little or no debt from a school that gave them real financial support is in a fundamentally better position than a student who graduates from a brand-name school carrying $80,000 or more in loans. The brand name opens some doors. The debt closes others. And the doors it closes, the ability to take a risk on a career they really care about, to move to a new city, to save money, to build financial stability in their twenties, are doors that matter enormously.

Think about a hypothetical parent named Amara, a 44-year-old who works as a hospital administrator and came to the US from Ghana twenty years ago. Her daughter Abena is a strong student with a 3.9 GPA and genuine talent in computer science. Abena got into a well-known private university and a state school with a strong tech program. The private university offered a small merit scholarship that brought the annual cost down to $42,000. The state school offered a larger merit award that brought the annual cost to $11,000. Amara's instinct was to push for the private school because the name felt more impressive to her and to her community. But when she finally ran the numbers, the difference in cost over four years was over $120,000. Abena chose the state school, graduated debt-free, and had the financial freedom to take an internship in a city she wanted to live in without worrying about loan payments. The name on the diploma mattered far less than the options that came with financial freedom.

The specific tool you need right now is the net price calculator. Every college in the United States that receives federal financial aid funding is required by law to have a net price calculator on their website. You can usually find it by searching the school's name plus "net price calculator." This tool asks you to enter basic financial information, your family's income, assets, household size, and the number of people in college, and it gives you an estimated annual cost after all grants and scholarships are applied. It's not a guarantee. The actual award letter may differ. But it gives you a realistic ballpark before your child applies, which is exactly when you need it.

Spend one evening this week running the net price calculator for every school currently on your child's list. Write down the estimated annual cost for each one. Then multiply by four. That's the rough total investment you're looking at for each school. Looking at those numbers side by side, before applications are submitted, changes everything about how you think about the list. Schools that looked similar suddenly look very different. Schools you hadn't considered might move up. Schools you were excited about might need a harder conversation. That's not a bad thing. That's exactly the information you need to make a smart decision.

One more concept worth understanding here is the difference between schools that meet full demonstrated need and schools that don't. Some colleges, mostly well-endowed private schools, commit to meeting 100% of every admitted student's demonstrated financial need. That means if their formula determines your family needs $30,000 in aid per year, they'll provide it. Other schools make no such commitment. They offer whatever they can afford to offer, which may cover a fraction of your need or none of it at all. Knowing which category a school falls into before your child applies is a real advantage. You can find this information on a school's financial aid page or by searching the school's name plus "meets full demonstrated need."

For example, let's say your family can contribute $10,000 a year toward college costs. Your in-state university, School A, is $25,000 a year if your child lives at home and $45,000 a year if they live on campus. Your need is $15,000 per year if they live at home ($25,000 – $10,000) or $35,000 ($45,000-$10,000) if they live on campus. Your in-state university school 'A' doesn't meet demonstrated need. Now let's look at school B. School B is a well-regarded private school in another state that costs $90,000 a year for a student living on campus. Your need for this school is $80,000 a year

($90,000 – $10,000). School B also is committed to meeting full demonstrated need without loans. *Here's what those numbers actually show:

	School A at home	School A on Campus	School B
	$25,000	$45,000	$90,000
Estimated Family Contribution (EFC)	$10,000	$10,000	$10,000
Demonstrated need	$15,000	$35,000	$80,000
Need fully met	No**	No**	100%; no loans
What you pay	$15,000	$35,000	$10,000
**Some schools meet partial need through loans. Always check each school's financial aid page.			

*Not every school that meets full demonstrated need does so without loans: read the fine print carefully.

For working-class and immigrant families, this information is especially important. Schools that meet full demonstrated need can sometimes be more affordable for lower-income families than public schools that don't offer much aid. A highly selective private university with a large endowment might end up costing a family earning $55,000 a year less than their in-state public university, because the private school has the resources to cover a much larger portion of the cost. This is counterintuitive, and it's one of the most important things most families never learn until it's too late to use it.

The FAFSA Demystified — What It Is, Why It Matters, and How to File It Right

The FAFSA is the Free Application for Federal Student Aid. It's a federal form that determines how much financial aid your child is eligible to receive from the federal government, from most states, and from most colleges. Without it, your child can't access federal grants, federal student loans, or work-study programs. Many colleges also use FAFSA data to calculate their own institutional aid awards. Filing it correctly and on time is one of the single most important financial actions you'll take in this entire process.

And yet millions of families either file it late, file it with errors, or don't file it at all.

The most common reason families skip it is the assumption that they won't qualify for aid because their income is too high. This assumption is wrong more often than most people realize. The FAFSA calculates something called the Student Aid Index, which is a number that represents what the government believes your family can contribute to college costs. That number is based on more than just income. It factors in family size, the number of people in college at the same time, certain assets, and other circumstances. Families with household incomes well into six figures sometimes qualify for meaningful aid, especially at schools with large endowments. You won't know until you file. And filing costs nothing.

The FAFSA typically opens on October 1st each year for the following academic year. That means if your child is starting college in the fall of 2026, the FAFSA opens on October 1st, 2025. File it as close to October 1st as possible. Because FAFSA dates can change, check the official opening date in early September. Many states and many colleges award aid on a first-come, first-served basis, meaning the earlier you file, the more aid may be available to your child. Waiting until spring to file is one of the most common and most costly mistakes families make. By the time a late filer submits their form, some aid pools are already depleted.

Here's exactly what you need to file the FAFSA. You need your Social Security number and your child's Social Security number. You need your federal tax return from the prior year, which is called the "prior-prior year" return in FAFSA language. If you're filing in October 2025, you'll use your 2024 tax return. You need records of any untaxed income, such as child support received or contributions to tax-deferred retirement accounts. You need bank account balances and the value of any investments you hold outside of retirement accounts. And you need your child's FSA ID, which is a username and password created on the StudentAid.gov website. Both you and your child need separate FSA IDs. Create them before you sit down to file, because the creation process can take a day or two to verify.

The most common mistakes on the FAFSA that cost families money are worth knowing specifically so you can avoid them. The first mistake is not reporting assets correctly. Some families forget to include savings accounts, investment accounts, or money held in a child's name. Others accidentally include retirement accounts, which are specifically excluded from FAFSA calculations. Read each question carefully. When in doubt, the FAFSA help text for each question explains exactly what should and shouldn't be included.

The second mistake is using the wrong tax year. The FAFSA uses your tax return from two years prior, not last year's return. This trips up a lot of families who try to use the most recent return and end up with errors that delay processing.

The third mistake is missing the deadline. Every state has its own FAFSA priority deadline, and many are earlier than families expect. Some state deadlines fall in February or March. A few fall even earlier. Go to the FAFSA website, click on "State Aid Deadlines," find your state, and write that date on your calendar right now. Your state's deadline is the one that matters most for state grant programs, and missing it can mean losing thousands of dollars in aid that doesn't carry over to the following year.

The fourth mistake is not updating the FAFSA if your financial situation changes. If a parent loses a job, if income drops significantly, or if there's a major financial hardship after the FAFSA is filed, contact the financial aid office at each school your child is considering and explain the situation. Schools have a process called professional judgment that allows financial aid administrators to adjust an aid award based on circumstances not reflected in the FAFSA. Most families don't know this exists. It can make a real difference.

After you file, you'll receive a Student Aid Report that summarizes what you submitted and shows your Student Aid Index. Review it carefully. If anything looks wrong, you can correct it by logging back into your FAFSA and making changes. Then each college your child listed on the FAFSA will receive your information and use it to calculate their aid offer, which will appear in the financial aid award letter that comes with or shortly after the acceptance letter.

One specific thing for immigrant families to know. You do not need to be a US citizen to file the FAFSA. Eligible non-citizens, including permanent residents with green cards, can file and qualify for federal aid. Undocumented students cannot file the federal FAFSA, but many states have their own state financial aid programs that are available regardless of immigration status, and many private colleges have their own institutional aid programs with no citizenship requirement. If this applies to your family, contact the financial aid office at each school your child is interested in and ask directly what aid is available to students in your child's situation. The answers will vary by school, and the only way to know is to ask.

The CSS Profile - What It Is and Who Needs It

Before we move on to merit aid and scholarships I want to make you aware of another financial aid form that some colleges and universities require you to file for institutional aid (that's aid from the school's money, not federal money). The dates are determined by each institution and that information will be on the school's financial aid page of their website.

Unlike the FAFSA, the CSS Profile is not free. There is a cost, but fee waivers are available for families with qualifying incomes. The CSS Profile may ask about:

- how much equity you have in your home
- how many cars you own and their value among other things.

Each school selects what CSS Profile questions it wants to ask from a large list. If your child is applying to more than one school that wants the CSS Profile, the questions from each school will be combined into one questionnaire for you to fill out. Each institution only receives the answers to their questions but that means your CSS Profile application can be anywhere from a few pages to much more. It's also important to know that some schools also require the non-custodial parent to file in cases of divorce or separation.

The CSS Profile can be found on College Board's website if you would like more information.

Merit Scholarships, Need-Based Aid, and the Difference Between Them

These two terms get used interchangeably by a lot of parents, and that confusion leads to missed money. They're different things, they work differently, and understanding both gives you a much clearer picture of where your child's financial help is actually likely to come from.

Need-based aid is financial assistance given based on your family's financial situation. It's calculated using your FAFSA data and is designed to help families who demonstrate financial need afford college. Need-based aid can come from the federal government in the form of Pell Grants, from your state through state grant programs, or from the college itself through institutional grants. The key thing to understand about need-based aid is that it's determined by a formula, not by your child's academic performance. A family with significant financial need whose child has a 3.0 GPA can qualify for the same need-based grant as a family with the same financial profile whose child has a 4.0 GPA.

Merit scholarships are different. They're awarded based on your child's academic achievement, test scores, talent, or other accomplishments, regardless of financial need. A family earning $200,000 a year can receive a merit scholarship. A student with a 3.5 GPA from a lower-income family might not qualify for certain merit awards if the threshold is higher. Merit scholarships are the college's way of attracting students they want, and understanding this is very important for building a smart college list.

Here's the part most families miss. Many colleges use merit scholarships strategically to recruit strong students who might otherwise choose a more prestigious school. A mid-tier school that really wants your child in their freshman class might offer a merit scholarship worth $15,000 or $20,000 a year to make attendance financially attractive. A highly selective school that receives 50,000 applications has less incentive to compete for any individual student with merit money. The result is that schools slightly below your child's academic level, schools where your child's GPA and test scores are above the school's typical range, are often the schools most likely to offer significant merit awards.

This is called being a "big fish in a smaller pond," and it's one of the most financially powerful strategies in college admissions that most families never use deliberately.

To find schools where your child is likely to be a strong merit scholarship candidate, look at each school's Common Data Set and find the middle 50% range for GPA and test scores among admitted students. If your child's numbers are at or above the top of that range, they're a strong candidate for merit money at that school. If your child's numbers fall in the middle of the range, they might get some merit aid but probably not the largest awards. If their numbers fall below the range, merit money is unlikely. This analysis takes about 20 minutes per school and gives you a realistic picture of where the financial opportunities are.

Outside scholarships are the other piece of this, and they're worth real effort even though many families underestimate what's actually available. Outside scholarships are awards given by organizations, foundations, companies, and community groups that are separate from the college itself. Some are large and nationally competitive. Others are small, local, and receive very few applications because nobody knows about them.

The small, local scholarships are often the most accessible. Your child's high school guidance office almost always has a list of local scholarships available to students in your area. Community foundations, local businesses, civic organizations like Rotary clubs, religious institutions, and professional associations in your field all frequently offer scholarships that go underutilized simply because students don't apply. A $1,000 scholarship might not feel transformative on its own, but three or four of them add up, and the application process for smaller scholarships is usually much less competitive than the large national ones.

For nationally competitive scholarships, the most well-known include the Gates Scholarship for high-achieving students from low-income backgrounds, the Coca-Cola Scholars Program, the Dell Scholars Program for first-generation college students, the Jack Kent Cooke Foundation scholarship, and the QuestBridge National College Match for high-achieving, low-income students. Each has specific eligibility requirements and application processes. Look them up, check the eligibility criteria against your child's profile, and add the applicable ones to your scholarship calendar.

Build a scholarship search calendar the same way you built the application deadline calendar. List every scholarship your child will apply for, the deadline, the requirements, and what materials are needed. Start working on applications at least six weeks before each deadline. Many scholarship applications require essays, and those essays deserve the same care as college application essays. A rushed scholarship essay is a wasted opportunity.

One important thing to know about outside scholarships: when your child receives one, they're required to report it to their college's financial aid office. Some schools reduce their own institutional aid dollar-for-dollar when outside scholarships come in, which can feel discouraging. Others allow outside scholarships to reduce the loan portion of the aid package first, which is honestly helpful. Ask each school's financial aid office directly how they treat outside scholarships before assuming the worst. The policy varies significantly from school to school.

How to Read and Compare Award Letters Like a Pro

When the acceptance letters arrive, they're almost always accompanied by financial aid award letters. And this is where a lot of families make an expensive mistake. They look at the bottom line number, assume it represents what they'll actually pay, and make a college decision based on a number that isn't what it appears to be.

Award letters are not standardized. Every school formats them differently. Some are clear and easy to read. Others are deliberately or accidentally confusing in ways that make a school look more affordable than it really is. Knowing how to read them accurately is a skill that could save your family tens of thousands of dollars.

The first thing to do with any award letter is separate the aid into two categories: money you don't have to pay back and money you do. Grants and scholarships are money you don't pay back. Loans are money you do. Work-study is money your child earns through a part-time campus job. It isn't money that has to be repaid, but it also isn't guaranteed free money, since students still need to apply for available positions at their school. For the latest information on work study and the FAFSA visit studentaid.gov or do a web search for Federal Student Aid(.gov).

Some award letters present all of these together under a heading like "Total Financial Aid Package," which can make the total look much larger and the school look much more affordable than it really is.

To compare award letters clearly, create two columns on a piece of paper:
- Free Money
- Money to Repay or Earn

Now subtract only the free money from the school's total cost of attendance. The number you're left with is the actual out-of-pocket cost for that school, the amount your family would need to cover through savings, income, or loans. That is the number that matters.

Cost of attendance includes more than tuition. It also includes housing, meals, books, transportation, and personal expenses. Always compare schools using the full cost of attendance, not just tuition, because a school with lower tuition can still end up costing more overall.

Once you've calculated the actual out-of-pocket cost for each school that sent an award letter, the comparison often produces surprises. A school that seemed expensive based on its sticker price might end up being the most affordable option after a large merit scholarship. A school that seemed affordable might have offered very little aid and in reality costs more than any other option on the list.

There's one more thing to check in every award letter: whether the aid is renewable. Some merit scholarships require students to maintain a certain GPA to keep the award each year. Read the renewal requirements carefully and ask questions if anything is unclear.

"Is this award renewable? What are the requirements to keep it?" are completely reasonable questions, and any financial aid office should answer them clearly.

Comparing award letters from different schools is also something you can do with a simple spreadsheet. Create one row for each school. Create columns for total cost of attendance, total grants and scholarships, total loans offered, total work-study offered, and the actual out-of-pocket cost after subtracting only grants and scholarships. Add a column for the renewal requirements on any merit awards. Seeing the numbers side by side makes the financial picture much clearer.

Negotiating financial aid is something most families don't know they can do, but many schools are willing to revisit an award under the right circumstances. If your child receives a significantly better offer from a comparable school, you can contact the financial aid office at the school your child prefers and ask whether they're able to revisit the award. This works more often than most families realize. The conversation should be polite, specific, and focused on facts. "We received an award letter from [comparable school] offering $X in grants. Our family's preference is to attend your school, and we wanted to ask if there's any flexibility in the award based on this competing offer." That's it. No drama, no demands. Just a clear, respectful ask with evidence behind it.

Having the Money Conversation With Your Teen Without Making It Weird

Money is one of the most avoided topics in family life. Most parents would rather talk about almost anything else. And that avoidance, when it comes to college, creates a specific and very painful problem. Your child applies to schools you can't afford, gets in, falls in love with the idea of going there, and then gets blindsided by a financial reality they didn't know existed. The disappointment is real. The resentment, sometimes directed at you, is real. And all of it was avoidable.

The conversation about money doesn't have to be heavy or scary. It just has to happen, and it has to happen early enough to matter.

The right time to have this conversation is before your child builds their college list, not after the acceptance letters arrive. That timing is everything. A teenager who knows the financial parameters before they start researching schools can factor that information into their choices from the beginning. A teenager who finds out the financial reality after they've already fallen in love with a school they can't afford experiences it as a loss, not as information.

Here's a specific script for starting this conversation in a way that doesn't feel like a lecture or a letdown. Find a calm moment, not during homework, not after a stressful day. Sit down together and say something like this: "I want to talk about how we're going to approach the college decision financially. I don't want you to feel limited, but I also want us to be honest with each other, so we're not surprised later. Here's what I know about what our family can realistically contribute each year. And here's what I want you to know about how financial aid and scholarships work, because there's actually more flexibility than most people realize."

That opening does several things at once. It signals that this is a conversation, not a pronouncement. It acknowledges your child's feelings before they have a chance to shut down. It introduces the financial reality without making it feel like a wall. And it opens the door to talking about the strategies, merit scholarships, financial aid, smart list-building, that can actually expand their options within your family's financial reality.

Be specific about what your family can contribute. Vague statements like "we can't afford an expensive school" don't give your child anything useful to work with. A specific number does. "We can realistically contribute around $X per year without taking on debt that would hurt our family" gives your child a concrete parameter. It doesn't limit where they can apply. It just means they need to look for schools where the aid makes the real cost work within that range. That's a solvable problem, and framing it that way changes the emotional tone of the conversation entirely.

For immigrant families, this conversation often carries extra weight. Many immigrant parents have sacrificed enormously and feel deeply that they should be able to give their child whatever school they want. Admitting a financial limit can feel like admitting that the sacrifice wasn't enough. It isn't that. It's honesty, and honesty protects your child from a financial situation that could follow them for decades.

You can honor everything you've sacrificed and still have a realistic conversation about what's affordable. In fact, that's exactly what the sacrifice was for: to give your child a real future, not a debt-loaded one.

For working-class families where money has always been tight, these conversations may feel more natural because financial limits have always been part of the picture. But there's a specific thing worth saying to your teenager in these families: the financial aid system was designed with you in mind. Federal Pell Grants exist specifically for students from lower-income families. Many of the most generous merit scholarship programs target first-generation college students and students from working-class backgrounds. Your family's financial situation is not a disadvantage in the financial aid process. In many ways, it's an advantage. Make sure your child understands that.

One practical thing to do together once you've had the initial money conversation: sit down with your child and run the net price calculator for three or four schools on their list together. Let them see the numbers in real time. Let them ask questions. Let them be part of the process of understanding what things actually cost and what aid might look like. A teenager who understands how financial aid works is a teenager who can be a real partner in building a college list that makes sense, instead of a passenger who gets surprised by the outcome.

Financial responsibility is a life skill. The teenager who learns to factor financial reality into a major decision, who understands the difference between a grant and a loan, who knows how to read a financial document and ask smart questions about it, that teenager is building exactly the kind of practical intelligence that serves people well in every financial decision they'll ever make. The college process is the first real opportunity most kids have to practice that skill. Use it.

Recap: What We Covered and Your Action Steps

This chapter covered five things that most families either learn too late or never learn at all. Understanding financial fit. Filing the FAFSA correctly and on time. Knowing the difference between merit scholarships and need-based aid and where to find both. Reading award letters accurately so you can compare actual costs instead of misleading totals. And having honest money conversations with your teenager before the pressure of decisions makes those conversations harder than they need to be.

Every one of these things is learnable. None of them require a financial background or a private counselor. They require your time and your willingness to treat the financial side of this process as seriously as the academic side.

Here are your specific action steps, in the order that makes sense to work through them.

This week, run the net price calculator for every school currently on your child's list. Write down the estimated annual out-of-pocket cost for each one and multiply by four. Look at those numbers side by side. Let them inform how you think about the list before applications are submitted.

Before October 1st of your child's senior year, create your FSA IDs on StudentAid.gov. Both you and your child need separate ones. Gather your most recent federal tax return, your bank account information, and your Social Security numbers. File the FAFSA as close to October 1st as possible. Look up your state's FAFSA priority deadline and write it on your calendar. Do not miss it.

In the next two weeks, identify three to five schools on your child's list where their GPA and test scores are at or above the top of the school's middle 50% admitted student range. These are your merit scholarship target schools. Research what merit awards each school offers, what the eligibility requirements are, and whether the awards are renewable. Add this information to your college comparison spreadsheet.

Ask your child's school counselor for a list of local scholarships available to students in your area. Also look up two or three of the national scholarship programs mentioned in this chapter that your child might qualify for. Build a scholarship calendar with every applicable deadline, what materials are needed, and a six-week lead time before each deadline to allow for essay writing and revisions.

Have the money conversation with your teenager before the college list is finalized. Use the script from this chapter as a starting point. Be specific about what your family can realistically contribute per year. Then run the net price calculator together for a few schools so your child understands how the numbers actually work. Make this a conversation, not a lecture, and leave room for questions.

When award letters arrive, use the two-column method to separate free money from money that needs to be repaid or earned. Build a comparison spreadsheet with the real out-of-pocket cost for each school. Check renewal requirements on every merit award. If a competing school has offered significantly better aid, contact the financial aid office at your preferred school and ask politely whether they're able to revisit the offer.

The teenager who goes through this process with a real understanding of how college finances work doesn't just make a smarter college decision. They walk into adult life knowing how to read a financial document, how to ask smart questions about money, and how to make major decisions with both their heart and their head. That combination is rare. And it starts with the conversations you're willing to have right now, before the pressure of the moment makes them harder than they need to be.

Chapter 7
Raising a Life-Ready Kid – The Skills, Mindsets, and Identity That Actually Determine Success

Everything covered in the previous six chapters, the grades, the test scores, the essays, the financial aid forms, all of it is preparation for something bigger. And that bigger thing isn't a college acceptance letter. It's a person. A person who can walk into an unfamiliar situation and figure it out. A person who knows who they are, what they care about, and how to keep going when things get hard. That's what you've actually been building this whole time, even if it didn't always feel that way.

This chapter is about making that explicit.

Because here's what the college prep process, done right, actually produces. Not just a strong application. Not just an acceptance letter. A teenager who has spent four years building self-awareness, developing real skills, taking on increasing responsibility, and learning to navigate a world that doesn't always go their way. That teenager doesn't just get into college. They thrive there. And they're far more prepared for every job, relationship, and hard situation that comes after.

The four sections in this chapter cover the parts of raising a life-ready kid that most college prep books skip entirely. Identity and self-awareness. Soft skills that make someone hireable. How to raise a self-directed teen without losing your mind. And social media, specifically how it can quietly open doors or close them before anyone ever reads an application. Each section gives you specific, actionable steps. Not vague encouragement. Real things to do, in a specific order, with a clear outcome.

The Identity Question Colleges Are Really Asking

Every college application has a surface layer and a deeper layer. The surface layer is the one most families focus on: grades, activities, test scores, recommendations. The deeper layer is the one that actually separates the applications that feel alive from the ones that feel assembled. And that deeper layer comes down to one question that runs through every essay, every activity description, every interview answer your child will ever give.

Who are you?

Not "what have you done." Not "what are your accomplishments." Who are you, what do you genuinely care about, and why does any of it matter to you? Admissions officers read thousands of applications every cycle, and they can feel the difference between a student who has actually thought about this and a student who hasn't. The student who hasn't tends to write essays that list achievements. The student who has tends to write essays that feel like a real person is on the page. One gets remembered. The other doesn't.

Self-awareness is the most underrated factor in college admissions. It's also the most underrated factor in long-term success. A person who knows who they are makes better decisions. They choose careers that actually fit them instead of careers that sound impressive. They know when to ask for help and when to push through on their own. They can describe themselves clearly in a job interview, in a difficult conversation, in any situation where someone needs to know what they're made of. That clarity doesn't come from nowhere. It gets built over years of paying attention to yourself.

Most teenagers haven't been asked to think about this in any serious way. School asks them to learn things and demonstrate knowledge. It rarely asks them to reflect on who they're becoming. Parents, especially busy ones, often skip this conversation because it feels abstract or because there's always something more urgent to deal with. So a lot of teenagers arrive at the college essay process unable to answer the question "who are you" in any meaningful way. And that's not their fault. Nobody helped them build that answer.

Your job, starting right now, is to help them build it.

Here's a specific exercise to do with your child this week. It takes about 45 minutes, and it works best when neither of you is rushed. Sit down together and go through these five questions. Ask your child to answer each one out loud while you write down what they say. Don't comment, don't edit, don't react. Just write:

1. What's something you've done in the last two years that you're genuinely proud of, not because someone else was impressed, but because you felt good about it yourself?
2. What's something you believe that most people your age don't seem to believe?
3. When have you felt most like yourself, doing what, and why?
4. What's something you've changed your mind about in the last year, and what changed it?
5. What's a problem in the world, your school, or your neighborhood that actually bothers you enough to want to do something about it?

When they're done, read back what you wrote. Then ask one follow-up: "Is there a thread you see connecting any of these answers?" If they can see it, great. If they can't, that's okay too. You're not looking for a finished identity. You're looking for the raw material that one is built from. Whatever surfaces in that conversation is real information about who your child is right now, and it's the foundation that every essay, every interview answer, and every meaningful conversation about their future can be built on.

Do this exercise once, then revisit it every few months with one or two of the same questions. Identity isn't static. A 15-year-old and a 17-year-old are different people, and the answers change. The habit of asking these questions builds the habit of self-reflection, which is itself the skill you're trying to develop. A teenager who regularly reflects on their own experience, who can articulate what they value and why, is a teenager who can answer the identity question that runs beneath every college application, and every job interview they'll ever face.

For immigrant families, this exercise sometimes surfaces something important that gets overlooked. Your child's experience of navigating between cultures, of holding two identities at once, of understanding things about the world that their peers have never had to think about, is not a complication. It's a perspective. And perspective, clearly articulated, is one of the most compelling things a college application can show. Help your child see their background not as something to explain or apologize for, but as something that really shaped how they see the world. That framing changes everything about how they write about themselves.

One more thing about identity that's worth saying directly. Your child doesn't need to have everything figured out. Colleges aren't looking for teenagers who have life completely sorted. They're looking for teenagers who are genuinely engaged in the process of figuring it out. A student who can say "I don't know exactly what I want to do yet, but here's what I care about and here's why it matters to me" is more compelling than a student who has a polished five-year plan that doesn't actually connect to anything real about who they are. Honesty beats certainty every single time.

The Soft Skills That Make Someone Hireable (And How High School Builds Them)

Ask any hiring manager what they wish new college graduates had more of, and you'll hear the same answers over and over. Not more technical knowledge. Not higher GPAs. Communication skills. The ability to solve problems without being told exactly what to do. Resilience when something doesn't go as planned. The basic willingness to show up consistently and follow through on commitments. These are the things that determine whether a person actually succeeds in their first job, and in every job after that.

None of them are taught in a classroom.

They're built through experience. Through situations where something is genuinely hard and the person has to figure out how to handle it. Through moments of failure that require recovery. Through the daily practice of doing things that matter even when it's inconvenient. High school is full of those moments, if you know how to use them.

Communication is the first skill worth building deliberately, and it's broader than most people think. It's not just about speaking clearly or writing well, though both of those matter. It's about knowing how to have a hard conversation without shutting down. It's about being able to ask for what you need. It's about listening well enough to actually understand what someone else is saying before responding. These are skills that take years to develop, and high school gives your child four years of daily practice opportunities if you frame them correctly.

Here's how to build communication skills into your child's everyday high school experience without adding anything to their plate. When your child has a conflict with a teacher over a grade, don't resolve it for them. Coach them on how to approach the conversation, then let them have it. When they have a disagreement with a friend, ask them what they said and what the other person said, and help them think through whether there was a better way to handle it. When they have to present something in class, ask them to practice it out loud at home first, not to perform for you, but to hear themselves say it. These aren't extra activities. They're the situations your child is already in. You're just using them intentionally.

Problem-solving is the second skill, and it's the one most parents accidentally undermine without realizing it. Every time you solve a problem for your child that they could have solved themselves, you rob them of a problem-solving experience. Not because you're a bad parent, but because you love them and it's faster and easier to just fix it. The result is a teenager who has never had to figure something out on their own, who gets to college and freezes when a problem appears that nobody is there to solve for them.

The fix is simple, but it requires discipline. When your child comes to you with a problem, your first response should be a question, not an answer. "What do you think you could do about that?" or "What have you already tried?" These questions aren't dismissive. They signal that you believe your child is capable of figuring this out, which is one of the most powerful things a parent can communicate. And they give your child the experience of working through a problem before reaching for outside help, which is exactly the skill they'll need in college and in every workplace they ever enter.

Resilience is the third skill, and it might be the most important one. Resilience isn't about never struggling. It's about how quickly and effectively you recover when you do. A resilient person gets a bad grade, feels disappointed, figures out what went wrong, and adjusts. A person without resilience gets a bad grade and either spirals or gives up. That difference, played out across a lifetime, determines more about a person's success than almost any other single factor.

Think about a hypothetical student named Diego, a 16-year-old whose parents came from Mexico and who has been working hard in school his whole life. In the fall of junior year, Diego takes AP Chemistry and fails his first two tests. He's never failed a test before. His immediate reaction is to want to drop the class. His father, a 44-year-old construction worker named Ernesto, has a choice in that moment. He can let Diego drop the class, which would protect him from the discomfort but teach him that difficulty is a reason to quit. Or he can sit with Diego, acknowledge that it's hard, ask what's not clicking, help him find a tutor, and encourage him to stay in and see what happens. Ernesto chooses the second path. Diego stays in the class, brings his grade up to a B by the end of the semester, and writes about that experience in his college essay in a way that genuinely impresses the admissions officers who read it. More importantly, he now knows he can handle something hard without falling apart. That knowledge goes with him everywhere.

Showing up consistently is the fourth skill, and it's the one that gets the least attention but matters enormously in the real world. Employers consistently say that the single biggest differentiator between employees who advance and employees who don't is reliability. Not brilliance. Not creativity. Showing up when they said they would, doing what they committed to doing, following through even when it's inconvenient. That habit gets built in high school through part-time jobs, through extracurricular commitments, through being a person who keeps their word to teachers, coaches, and teammates.

If your child has a part-time job, treat it as a skill-building opportunity, not just a source of spending money. Ask them what they learned this week at work. Ask them about a situation that was hard and how they handled it. Ask them how they manage their time across school and work. These conversations make the skill-building visible and help your child connect their everyday experiences to the larger picture of who they're becoming.

Here's a simple monthly practice to build all four of these skills simultaneously. At the end of each month, sit down with your child for 20 minutes and ask three questions.

- First: what's something this month where you had to communicate something difficult?
- Second: what's a problem you solved on your own that you might have asked for help with before?
- Third: what's something that didn't go the way you planned, and what did you do with that?

These questions, asked consistently over the course of high school, do two things at once. They build the habit of reflection that produces self-awareness. And they generate the real-life material that college essays and job interviews are built from. A teenager who can answer these questions clearly and specifically is a teenager who is actually ready for what comes next.

How to Raise a Self-Directed Teen Without Losing Your Mind

The goal was never a teenager who does everything you tell them. The goal was always a teenager who can set a goal, make a plan, and follow through on their own. Those are two very different things, and the path between them requires something that most parents frankly find difficult: letting go of control in small, deliberate ways, starting much earlier than feels comfortable.

Self-direction doesn't appear on graduation day. It gets built gradually, over years, through a series of experiences where a young person is given real responsibility and then allowed to succeed or fail based on their own choices. The parents who raise self-directed teenagers are the ones who understood that their job was to gradually transfer ownership of their child's life back to their child, starting in 9th grade and completing the transfer by the time they leave home.

That transfer has a specific shape, and it looks different at each grade level.

In 9th grade, your child should own their homework schedule. Not with you reminding them every evening, but with a system they manage themselves, with your help setting it up initially. They should be making their own decisions about extracurricular activities, with your input but not your override. They should be communicating with their teachers directly when they have a question or concern, with your coaching beforehand if needed. Your role at this stage is consultant, not manager. You're available when asked. You're not hovering.

In 10th grade, your child should own their course selection process. They should be researching options, talking to their counselor, and bringing a recommendation to you rather than waiting for you to decide. They should be managing their own test prep schedule if they're doing any. They should be handling their own conflicts with peers and teachers without you as the first line of defense. Your role shifts further. You're a sounding board now, not a problem-solver.

In 11th grade, your child should own the college research process. They should be the one looking up schools, running net price calculators, and building the initial list. They should be managing their own application timeline, with you reviewing and supporting but not driving. They should be writing their own essays without you rewriting them. Your role is now support staff. You provide resources, you ask good questions, and you stay out of the driver's seat.

In 12th grade, your child should own the final decisions. Which school to attend. Which offer to accept. These decisions should be made by your child, with your honest input, not by you with your child's reluctant agreement. If your child owns the decision, they own the outcome. And a teenager who owns their college choice arrives on campus motivated in a way that a teenager who was placed there by their parents simply isn't.

The hardest part of this transfer isn't knowing what to hand over. It's watching your child struggle with what you've handed them without jumping in to rescue them.

That instinct to rescue is powerful, and it comes from love. But every time you rescue your child from a difficulty they could have handled themselves, you send a message you don't mean to send: I don't think you can do this. That message, received repeatedly over years, produces a teenager who genuinely doesn't believe they can do things on their own. Which then makes the rescue feel necessary, which reinforces the pattern.

It's a cycle, and the only way to break it is to let your child handle small things, even imperfectly, while the stakes are still low.

Accountability without nagging is the other piece of this, and it's something most parents struggle with because nagging feels like involvement and silence feels like neglect. The difference is actually about who owns the responsibility. When you nag, you're taking ownership of your child's responsibilities. When you hold them accountable, you're returning ownership to them while making the consequences clear.

Here's the specific difference in practice. Nagging sounds like: "Did you study for your test? You need to study for your test. Have you studied yet? Why haven't you studied?" Accountability sounds like: "We agreed you'd study for your chemistry test this week. What's your plan?" One question. Then silence. If they have a plan, great. If they don't, that's information. The consequence of not studying is a bad grade, not a lecture from you. The bad grade is the accountability. Your job is to make sure the consequence is allowed to land rather than being softened or prevented by your intervention.

Letting your child fail in small, safe ways is one of the most loving things you can do as a parent. A student who fails a quiz in 9th grade and learns from it is building resilience. A student who was protected from every small failure in high school and then fails for the first time at 19, alone, with no one to help them recover, is in a genuinely dangerous position. The small failures at home are the training ground. Don't eliminate them. Use them.

Here's a practical responsibility handoff timeline you can start using today, organized by what to transfer and when.

This month, identify one thing you're currently doing for your child that they could do themselves. It might be emailing a teacher about an assignment. It might be scheduling a dentist appointment. It might be tracking their own homework due dates. Pick one thing and hand it over completely. Tell your child clearly: "This is yours to manage now. I'm here if you have questions, but I'm not going to remind you." Then don't remind them. Whatever happens is part of the learning.

Each semester, add one more responsibility to the list. By the end of 10th grade, your child should be managing their own schedule, their own teacher communication, and their own extracurricular commitments without daily reminders from you. By the end of 11th grade, they should be leading the college research process, managing their own test prep, and handling their own conflicts and challenges independently. By the end of 12th grade, they should be the primary decision-maker about their own future, with you as an informed, supportive presence rather than the person running the show.

This process is uncomfortable. There will be moments when you see something going wrong and everything in you wants to step in. Sometimes you should, when the stakes are high and the harm is real. But most of the time, the discomfort you're feeling is not a sign that your child is in danger. It's a sign that they're learning. And learning sometimes looks messy from the outside.

Social Media — How It Can Help or Hurt Your Child's Future

Colleges Google applicants. Employers Google candidates. This is not a rumor or an occasional practice. It's a standard part of how institutions evaluate people before they make decisions. What shows up in that search can quietly open doors or close them before anyone ever reads a resume or an application. And most teenagers, and many parents, treat their child's online presence as something entirely separate from the college and career process. It isn't.

The digital footprint your child is building right now, every post, every comment, every photo, every public interaction, is part of their story whether they intended it to be or not.

The negative side of this is the part most parents have heard about. The offensive joke from 8th grade that's still publicly visible. The photo from a party that shows something no college admissions officer needs to see. The argument in a comment section that reveals a side of your child they'd never show in an interview. These things happen, and they have real consequences. Admissions offices at selective schools have rescinded acceptances over social media content. Employers have withdrawn job offers. These aren't hypothetical risks. They're documented outcomes that happen to real students every year.

But the positive side of this is the part most families completely miss, and it's actually more important for your child's future than the risk management piece.

Social media, used with intention and awareness, can be a real asset. A student who uses their online presence to document a real passion, to share work they're proud of, to build a visible record of who they are and what they care about, is doing something that most of their peers aren't. They're creating a positive digital footprint that supports their application instead of undermining it. An admissions officer who Googles a student and finds a thoughtful blog about environmental science, or a portfolio of original artwork, or a small YouTube channel where the student explains complex topics in their area of expertise, sees something that adds depth to the application rather than raising questions about the student's judgment.

The first step is a social media audit, and it needs to happen now, not the week before applications are due. Here's exactly how to do it.

Sit down with your child and spend one hour going through every platform they use. Instagram. TikTok. X (formerly Twitter). Snapchat public stories. YouTube. Facebook if they use it. Any forums or public comment sections where they post under their real name. For each platform, ask three questions: Is this account public or private? What would someone think of my child if this was the first thing they saw? Is there anything here that I'd be uncomfortable with an admissions officer or employer seeing?

For anything that raises a concern, the action is immediate. Delete the post or comment. Set the account to private if the content is personal and not meant for a public audience. For anything that's genuinely problematic, such as content that's offensive, that shows illegal activity, or that could be read as threatening or discriminatory, remove it entirely and do it today. Don't wait. The longer it stays up, the longer it's findable.

After the cleanup, talk with your child about what their digital presence currently says about them and what they'd want it to say. This isn't about creating a fake version of themselves online. It's about being intentional.

The same way you'd think about what to wear to an interview, you can think about what to post publicly. Not every post needs to be professional or college-related. But every public post should be something your child would be comfortable with a stranger seeing, because strangers are seeing it.

Now, the opportunity side. If your child has a real interest or passion, social media is one of the most accessible ways to build a visible record of that interest. A student who is passionate about astronomy and starts a simple Instagram account where they share what they're learning, photos they've taken, or explanations of concepts they find interesting, is doing several things at once. They're deepening their own knowledge by having to explain things clearly. They're building a public record of a genuine interest that supports their application story. And they're developing communication skills by learning to explain complex ideas in accessible ways. None of that requires a large following or professional-quality content. It requires consistency and authenticity, which are exactly the qualities that make it valuable.

LinkedIn is worth a specific mention for students who are 16 or older. A LinkedIn profile, built thoughtfully, gives your child a professional online presence that shows up in searches and that they can use actively when applying for internships, scholarships, and eventually jobs. A strong student LinkedIn profile includes a clear, professional photo, a brief summary that describes who they are and what they're interested in, their school and expected graduation year, any significant activities or projects, and any awards or recognitions. It doesn't need to be long. It needs to be accurate, professional, and present. Many internship and scholarship programs look at LinkedIn profiles as part of the application process, and a student who has one already is simply more visible than one who doesn't.

Here's a specific four-step plan for managing your child's digital presence from now through the college application process:

Step one: Do the audit together this week. Every platform, every account, using the three questions listed above. Handle anything concerning immediately.

Step two: Decide together which platforms will stay public and which will go private. As a general rule, anything that's primarily personal and social should be private. Anything that's being used to document a real interest or passion can stay public, with the understanding that it will be maintained thoughtfully.

Step three: If your child has a genuine interest they want to document publicly, help them choose one platform to do that on consistently. Not three platforms done half-heartedly. One platform, updated regularly, with content that reflects who they actually are. Consistency matters more than volume.

Step four: Set up a Google Alert for your child's name. Go to Google Alerts, enter your child's full name in quotes, and set it to notify you when new content appears online with that name. This takes two minutes and means you'll know immediately if something shows up in a search that you weren't aware of. Do this now, before applications go out, so you have time to address anything that surfaces.

The broader lesson here is one your child will use for the rest of their life. Every platform they post on, every comment they make publicly, every piece of content they put into the world with their name attached, is part of how the world sees them. That's not a reason to be paranoid or to stop using social media. It's a reason to use it with awareness and intention. A person who understands that their digital presence is part of their professional identity, and who manages it accordingly, has a real advantage in a world where everyone is searchable and first impressions happen before anyone ever picks up the phone.

What We Covered and Your Action Steps

This chapter was about the parts of raising a life-ready kid that don't show up on a transcript but determine everything about whether your child actually thrives once they leave home. Self-awareness and identity. Soft skills that make someone hireable. The gradual transfer of ownership and responsibility from you to your teenager. And a clear-eyed approach to social media that turns a potential liability into a genuine asset.

None of these things are separate from the college prep process. They're woven through every part of it. The teenager who knows who they are writes a better essay. The teenager who has built real communication and problem-solving skills has better interviews and better recommendations. The teenager who owns their own process shows up to college motivated in a way that can't be manufactured. And the teenager who manages their digital presence with intention arrives at the application process with nothing to hide and something real to show.

Here are your specific action steps, organized so you can start immediately and build from there.

This week, do the identity reflection exercise with your child. Set aside 45 minutes, ask the five questions, write down the answers without commenting, and then look for the thread connecting them. Save what comes out of that conversation. It's the raw material for every essay, every interview, and every meaningful conversation about your child's future.

Also this week, do the social media audit together. Every platform, the three questions, and immediate action on anything concerning. Set up the Google Alert for your child's name before you close your laptop.

Over the next month, identify one responsibility you're currently managing for your child that they could manage themselves. Hand it over completely, with a clear conversation about the transfer. Then let them own it, including the consequences if they don't follow through.

Once a month for the rest of high school, ask your child the three monthly reflection questions: a hard communication moment, a problem they solved independently, and something that didn't go as planned and what they did with it. Keep these conversations casual. The goal is the habit of reflection, not a formal debrief.

If your child is 16 or older, help them build a basic LinkedIn profile this month. A basic profile should include a professional photo, a short summary, school activities, and any relevant awards. Keep it simple. Make sure it's accurate and professional. Then leave it alone until there's something new worth adding.

The work you do in this chapter doesn't produce results you can see on a grade report or a test score. It produces a person. A person who knows themselves, who can handle hard things, who shows up consistently, and who takes responsibility for their own choices. That person doesn't just get into college. They build a life worth living once they get there. And that was always the real goal, from the very first page of this book to right here, right now.

Chapter 8
The Parent's Role – How to Be Supportive Without Taking Over

There's a moment most parents recognize. You're sitting across from your teenager, you've just brought up something about school or college, and within thirty seconds the conversation is over. Not because you said anything wrong. Not because your child is a bad kid. But because something in the way it landed felt like pressure, and they shut the door before it could go any further.

That moment happens in almost every family going through this process. And it almost always comes from the same place: a parent who loves their child deeply, who wants the best for them, and who has no idea that the way they're showing up is making things harder instead of easier.

This chapter is about that gap. The gap between what you intend and what your child actually experiences. Between being involved and being overbearing. Between supporting your teenager and slowly taking over a process that was supposed to be theirs. It's one of the most important ideas in this entire book, and it's also one of the most uncomfortable, because it requires you to look honestly at your own behavior without the protection of good intentions.

Good intentions don't automatically produce good outcomes. But awareness does. And that's exactly what this chapter gives you.

The Difference Between a Supportive Parent and a Controlling One

Most parents who are controlling don't think of themselves that way. They think of themselves as involved. Engaged. Doing what a good parent does when the stakes are high. And in many ways, that's true. The problem isn't the caring. The problem is what the caring looks like from the other side of the table.

Supportive and controlling can look almost identical from the outside. Both involve showing up. Both involve asking questions. Both involve caring deeply about the outcome. The difference is in who the process belongs to.

A supportive parent helps their child think through decisions. A controlling parent makes the decisions and hands them to their child to execute. A supportive parent asks questions that open things up. A controlling parent asks questions that are really just statements in disguise. A supportive parent lets their child struggle with something hard and stays nearby without jumping in. A controlling parent can't tolerate the struggle and fixes it before the lesson has a chance to land.

This distinction matters enormously in the college process, because this is the first time in most teenagers' lives where the work is genuinely theirs to own. The essay has to come from them. The choice of schools has to reflect what they actually want. The motivation to push through a hard semester has to come from inside, not from a parent standing over their shoulder reminding them what's at stake. A teenager who has been managed through every step of this process arrives at college having never actually owned any of it. And that's when things fall apart.

Let's look at another parent named Sunita, a 46-year-old who came to the US from India in her twenties and built a career in accounting through sheer determination. Her daughter Priya is a junior with strong grades and a genuine interest in environmental policy. Sunita loves her daughter fiercely and has sacrificed a great deal to give her opportunities she never had. But Sunita also checks Priya's grades online three times a week, edits every essay before Priya considers it finished, has already identified the colleges she thinks Priya should attend, and brings up the college process in almost every conversation they have. Priya has started lying about small things, telling her mother the essay is done when it isn't, saying she already talked to her counselor when she hasn't, just to create breathing room. She's not a dishonest kid. She's a kid who has learned that the only way to have any ownership over her own life is to manage the information her mother receives. That's not a healthy dynamic. And it didn't happen because Sunita is a bad parent. It happened because love, without boundaries, becomes control.

Here's a quick self-check you can do right now, honestly and without judgment. Read through these statements and notice which ones feel familiar.

- You check your child's grades online more than once a week without them asking you to.
- You've rewritten or heavily edited something your child wrote for school or for an application.
- You've contacted a teacher, coach, or counselor about something your child could have handled themselves.
- You bring up college in more than half of your conversations with your teenager.
- You feel physically anxious when your child doesn't immediately respond to a question about school or their future.
- You've already decided which colleges are on the list and you're working to get your child to agree.

None of these things make you a bad parent. Every single one of them comes from love. But if several of them felt familiar, that's useful information. It tells you where the line between involved and controlling has been crossed, and it gives you a specific place to start pulling back.

The shift from controlling to supportive isn't about caring less. It's about trusting more. Trusting that your child is capable of handling this, with your support, on their own terms. That trust is not blind. It's built over time, through the gradual handover of responsibility we talked about in Chapter 7. But it has to be real. A teenager can feel the difference between a parent who genuinely believes in them and a parent who says they believe in them while quietly managing every outcome. One of those experiences builds confidence. The other quietly erodes it.

The most practical shift you can make right now is this: change the ratio of questions to statements in your conversations about college. For every statement you make about what your child should do, replace it with a genuine question about what they think. "What do you think about that school?" instead of "I think you should apply there." "What's your plan for the essay this week?" instead of "You need to work on your essay this week." The content of the conversation doesn't change much. The ownership does. And ownership is everything.

Scripts and Strategies for the Conversations That Actually Matter

Knowing what to say is one thing. Knowing how to say it, and when, is something else entirely. The college prep process produces a specific set of conversations that most parents dread, not because they don't care, but because they know from experience that these conversations can go sideways fast. Grades. Rejection. Giving up. Success that comes with pressure attached. Each of these moments is an opportunity to either strengthen your relationship with your teenager or damage it. The difference, more often than not, comes down to specific words and specific timing.

The grade conversation is the one that happens most often and goes wrong most reliably. You see a grade you're not happy with. Your first instinct is to say something. And the way that something gets said determines whether your child opens up or shuts down for the next three days.

The version that doesn't work sounds like this: "Did you see your grade in history? That's not good. You need to study more. What happened? Are you even trying?" Every sentence in that sequence, even though it comes from genuine concern, lands as an accusation. Your child hears: you failed, I'm disappointed, and I don't think you're trying hard enough. The defensive wall goes up immediately, and you've lost the conversation before it started.

The version that works sounds like this: "I saw your history grade. I'm not going to pretend I didn't notice. Can you tell me what's going on in that class?" Then stop. Don't fill the silence. Don't add "because I'm worried" or "because you need to do better." Just ask the question and wait. That pause is where your child decides whether to actually talk to you. If you fill it with more words, you've answered for them and the conversation is over. If you hold it, you've created space for something real.

After they respond, whatever they say, your next move is to reflect it back before you react to it. "So it sounds like the reading load is really heavy and you're having trouble keeping up with it. Is that right?" This does something important. It tells your child that you heard them, not just the grade, but what's actually going on. Once a person feels heard, they're far more open to problem-solving. You can ask "what do you think would help?" and actually get a real answer, instead of a shrug.

The rejection conversation is the hardest one, and it's the one parents prepare for the least. A college rejection hits your child in a place that's genuinely tender. They put work into that application. They imagined themselves there. They may have told people they applied. And now someone has looked at all of that and said no. The pain is real, and it deserves to be treated as real.

The instinct most parents have in that moment is to minimize it. "It's okay, there are other schools." "They don't know what they're missing." "Everything happens for a reason." These responses, however well-intentioned, tell your child that their feelings are too big and need to be fixed quickly. They don't feel comforting. They feel dismissive.

The script that actually helps sounds like this: "That's really disappointing. I know you wanted that one. I'm sorry." Full stop. Nothing after that. Not a silver lining. Not a pivot to the next school. Just acknowledgment. Let it sit for a moment. Then, only after your child has had space to feel it, you can ask: "Do you want to talk about it, or do you just need some time?" That question gives them control over what happens next, which is exactly what they need in a moment when something important just happened to them and they had no control over the outcome.

Give it at least a day before you bring up next steps. A teenager who is still sitting with a rejection is not ready to hear about the other schools on their list. When they are ready, which they'll signal by bringing it up themselves or by seeming more settled, you can have the forward-looking conversation. "Of everything else you applied to, which ones are you actually excited about?" That question redirects without dismissing. It opens a door without pushing your child through it.

The "I want to give up" conversation is one that catches parents off guard because it often comes at the worst possible moment, deep in junior year, or right before a big deadline, when there's no time to let them quit. Your child says something like "I don't even care about college anymore" or "I'm just going to take a year off" or "none of this matters." Your first instinct is probably to panic and argue. Don't.

What's almost always happening in those moments isn't a real decision. It's exhaustion talking. Your child is overwhelmed, and "I quit" is the emotional release valve. What usually makes things worse is treating it as if it's a real plan, either by arguing against it or by immediately agreeing to it. Both responses take the statement more literally than it was meant.

The script that works here is: "It sounds like you're really burned out right now. That makes sense. What's feeling like the most impossible thing at the moment?" That question moves the conversation from the abstract threat to quit to the specific thing that's actually overwhelming them. Once you know what that specific thing is, you can help them break it into smaller pieces. You're not solving it for them. You're helping them see that it's solvable.

The win conversation is one most parents don't think to prepare for, but it matters more than people realize. Your child gets a great test score, or gets into a school they wanted, or finishes an essay they're proud of. You celebrate. And then, in the same breath, you say something like "now you just need to keep that up" or "imagine if you'd done that all along" or "see what you can do when you really try." The celebration lands. And then the pressure lands right behind it. Your child learns, over time, that wins are never just wins. They're always the baseline for the next expectation.

The script for celebrating without adding pressure is simple: celebrate completely, and then stop. "That score is great. You worked hard for that and it shows. I'm proud of you." Period. No follow-up. No pivot to what comes next. Let the win be a win for a full day before anything else enters the conversation. A teenager who gets to experience genuine, uncomplicated pride in their own accomplishment is a teenager who builds intrinsic motivation. That motivation is what carries them through the hard parts when you're not there to push.

One practical tool worth making: a small card, index card size, with three or four of these scripts written on it in your own shorthand. Keep it somewhere easy to revisit, like your phone notes. Not because you'll read it mid-conversation, but because having reviewed it recently means the right words are closer to the surface when you need them. The conversations that matter most rarely happen when you're fully prepared. A little preparation goes a long way.

Letting Go — The Hardest and Most Important Thing You'll Do

Everything in this book has been building toward this. The grades, the essays, the financial aid, the skills, the identity work, all of it has one ultimate purpose. To produce a young person who can stand on their own. And the only way that happens is if you let them.

Letting go is not a single moment. It's not the day you drop them off at college or the day the acceptance letter arrives. It's a practice that starts in 9th grade and deepens every year until they leave. By the time move-in day comes, letting go should feel like the natural conclusion of a process that's been underway for four years, not a sudden, terrifying leap into the unknown.

But for many parents, especially the ones who love hardest, it doesn't feel that way. It feels like abandonment. It feels like giving up. It feels like if you stop watching closely, something will go wrong and it will be your fault for not catching it.

That fear is understandable. For immigrant parents who sacrificed enormously to create opportunities for their children, the stakes feel existential. Every stumble feels like a threat to everything they worked for. For working-class parents who know firsthand what happens when things fall apart without a safety net, stepping back feels reckless.

For all parents who have been deeply involved from the beginning, the identity of "involved parent" has become part of who they are. Letting go feels like losing a part of themselves.

All of those feelings are real. And none of them change what the research consistently shows: the students who thrive in college are the ones who learned to handle things on their own while they still had a safety net at home. Not the ones whose parents managed every outcome. The ones whose parents trusted them enough to let them struggle, fail, recover, and figure it out. That experience, repeated across four years of high school, produces a person who knows they can handle what comes next. There is no shortcut to that knowledge. It can only be earned through experience.

Letting go doesn't mean disappearing. It means changing your role. You move from manager to mentor. From problem-solver to sounding board. From the person who makes things happen to the person who believes your child can make things happen. That belief, expressed consistently and genuinely, is one of the most powerful things you can give them.

Here's what the emotional process of letting go actually looks like, because most books skip this part and it's the part that's hardest to navigate alone.

The first stage is resistance. You know intellectually that your child needs more independence, but every time you try to step back, something happens that pulls you back in. They miss a deadline. They make a choice you wouldn't have made. They don't seem to be taking something seriously enough. And you step in, because it feels like the responsible thing to do. This stage is normal. It doesn't mean you're failing at letting go. It means you're human and you love your child.

The second stage is discomfort. You've started stepping back more deliberately, and it feels genuinely uncomfortable. You're watching your child navigate something imperfectly and you're not jumping in to fix it. You're sitting with the anxiety of not knowing exactly what's happening at every moment. This discomfort is not a sign that something is wrong. It's a sign that you're doing something right. The discomfort is the feeling of trust being built.

The third stage is evidence. Your child handles something you thought they couldn't. They solve a problem without your help. They have a hard conversation with a teacher on their own. They recover from a setback faster than you expected. Each of these moments is evidence that your trust is warranted.

Collect that evidence. Remind yourself of it when the anxiety comes back, because it will.

The fourth stage is confidence. Not certainty, but confidence. You've seen your child handle enough things on their own that you genuinely believe they can handle what comes next. You're still there. You still care just as much. But you're no longer the one holding everything together. They are. And that's exactly what you were always working toward.

For parents who are worried that stepping back means their child will stop trying, here's something worth sitting with. A teenager who works hard because their parent is watching will stop working the moment the parent stops watching. That's not motivation. That's compliance. A teenager who works hard because they've connected their effort to something they genuinely care about will keep going whether you're watching or not. Your job isn't to be the reason they try. Your job is to help them find their own reason. Once they have it, they don't need you to manage them. They need you to believe in them. That's a very different kind of presence, and it's one you can sustain for the rest of their life.

Letting go looks like love when it's done right. It looks like saying "I trust you to handle this" and meaning it. It looks like being available without being ever-present. It looks like asking "how can I help?" instead of "here's what you need to do." It looks like celebrating their wins as theirs, not as evidence of your parenting. It looks like letting them own their failures without rushing to fix or explain them away.

The student who walks onto a college campus having been genuinely trusted by their parent is a different person than the one who was managed to the finish line. They know themselves. They've handled hard things. They've made real decisions and lived with the outcomes. They're not starting college hoping someone will tell them what to do. They're starting it knowing, from real experience, that they can figure it out.

That's the kid you've been raising this whole time. Not the kid with the best application. The kid who's ready for what comes after.

Putting It Into Practice — Your Personal Parenting Audit

This chapter asked you to look honestly at yourself, which is harder than looking at your child's transcript or their test scores. It asked you to consider whether the way you show up is helping or hurting. Whether your love is building your child up or quietly making them dependent. Whether you're ready to trust them with the thing you care most about, which is their own future.

That's not a comfortable set of questions. But they're the right ones.

Here are four specific actions to take, in order, starting this week:

First, do the self-check from the first section of this chapter with complete honesty. Go back and read the six statements again. Write down the ones that felt true. Don't judge yourself for what you write. Just be accurate. Then pick the one behavior on your list that you think has the most impact on your child's sense of ownership over their own process. That's the first thing to change. Not all of them at once. One specific behavior changed consistently, for the next thirty days.

Second, choose one conversation you've been avoiding or handling badly and prepare for it using the scripts from this chapter. Write out what you want to say in your own words, using the structure from the relevant script as a guide. Practice it out loud once, alone, so the words feel natural rather than rehearsed. Then have the conversation within the next week, in the right setting, at the right moment. Not forced. Not scheduled. But ready.

Third, identify one area where you're currently doing something for your child that they could do themselves. It might be checking their grades and reporting back to them. It might be managing their scholarship application deadlines. It might be editing their writing before they consider it done. Pick one thing and hand it over completely this week. Have a direct conversation about the transfer: "This is yours to manage now. I'm here if you need to think something through, but I'm not going to be tracking it for you." Then follow through on that. Whatever happens is part of their learning.

Fourth, create a simple weekly check-in structure that keeps you connected without hovering. Once a week, at a consistent time that works for both of you, spend fifteen minutes together. Not reviewing grades. Not going through a checklist. Just asking two questions: "What's going well this week?" and "Is there anything you want to think through together?"

That's it. Fifteen minutes. Two questions. The first question builds the habit of noticing what's working, which teenagers rarely do on their own. The second question keeps the door open for real conversations without forcing them. Over time, this check-in becomes the container for the relationship, the regular, low-pressure space where your child knows they can bring things to you without it turning into a crisis management session.

The parent who finishes this chapter and actually does these four things will have a different relationship with their teenager within thirty days. Not a perfect relationship. Not one without friction or worry. But one where the teenager feels genuinely trusted, where conversations about hard things are possible, and where the college process belongs to the right person.

That teenager doesn't just have a better shot at a strong application. They have a parent who believes in them.

Conclusion

The Real Win Was Never the Acceptance Letter

Four years. That's what this whole book has been about. Four years of habits, conversations, decisions, and small moments that add up to something much bigger than a college application. And now, standing at the end of it, the thing worth saying most clearly is this: if you've been doing this right, the acceptance letter was never the point.

The point was always the kid.

Think about what your child actually built between 9th grade and 12th grade if you followed the path laid out in these chapters. They learned to manage their own time without someone standing over them. They learned to advocate for themselves with teachers, counselors, and eventually admissions offices. They learned to recover from setbacks without falling apart. They found something they genuinely cared about and went deeper into it. They learned to tell a coherent, honest story about who they are. They handled rejection. They made real decisions and lived with the outcomes. They built skills that no test score can measure, and no transcript can fully capture.

That's not just a college applicant. That's a person who's ready for life.

The college admissions process, done the way this book describes it, is one of the most powerful frameworks for growing an adult that exists. Not because the process itself is perfect, it isn't. Not because every outcome is fair, it's not always. "But because the demands it places on a young person — know yourself, tell your story, show what you've done with your time, and handle the answer whatever it is — are the exact same demands that adult life places on everyone, every day, forever. A teenager who has genuinely worked through that process isn't just prepared for college. They're prepared for everything that comes after it.

That's the real win. Not the bumper sticker. Not the name of the school. The person who walks across the graduation stage carrying everything they built in these four years.

Those things don't disappear when the acceptance letter arrives. They don't disappear when the first semester of college starts, or when the first job offer comes in, or when the first really hard adult moment lands. They go everywhere. Every habit your child built around managing their own time will show up in how they handle a demanding job. Every time they practiced advocating for themselves with a teacher is practice for advocating for themselves with a manager. Every setback they recovered from in high school is evidence, evidence they carry inside them, that they can recover from the next one too.

You gave them that. Not by doing it for them. By creating the conditions where they could build it themselves.

That's what good parenting through this process actually looks like. Not managing every outcome. Not writing the essays. Not making the decisions. Showing up consistently, staying curious about your child as a person, holding the space for them to struggle and grow, and trusting them more and more as the years went on. That's the work.

Some parents reading this will have a child who got into their first-choice school. Some will have a child who landed somewhere they didn't expect. Some are reading this early enough that none of those outcomes have happened yet. It doesn't matter where you are in the timeline. The truth underneath all of it stays the same: the school your child attends is one chapter. The person they've become by the time they get there is the whole story.

And that story is already being written, right now, in the daily choices and habits and conversations happening in your house.

The Future Is Already Being Built — Start Now

Every week of high school is either building something or missing an opportunity to build it. That's not meant to scare you. It's meant to clarify something that gets lost in the noise of grades and deadlines and other parents' anxiety. The work of raising a life-ready kid isn't a sprint that starts in 11th grade. It's a slow, consistent accumulation of small things done well over four years.

The good news is that you now have everything you need to make sure those four years count.

You understand how modern college admissions actually works, not the version from ten years ago or the version other parents are guessing at, but the real one. You know what holistic review means and how to use it to your child's advantage. You know the difference between a well-rounded student and a student with a genuine spike, and you know which one actually stands out. You know how to build a college list that's smart instead of just hopeful.

You know what 9th grade is really for. You know why 10th grade is the most underused year in high school and how to change that. You know what junior year demands and how to sequence your attention, so the year feels like a plan instead of a panic. You know how to get through senior year without losing your relationship with your teenager in the process.

You know how to talk about money without making it a crisis. You know how to read an award letter accurately, how to file the FAFSA on time, and how to find merit scholarship opportunities that most families walk right past. You know the difference between a grant and a loan, and you know how to have the financial conversation with your teenager before the acceptance letters make it painful.

You know how to help your child build self-awareness, communication skills, resilience, and the ability to show up consistently, not by adding extra programs to their schedule, but by using the experiences they're already having. You know how to manage their digital footprint intentionally. You know how to raise a self-directed teenager without losing your mind or your relationship with them.

And you know, maybe most importantly, when to step back.

That last one is the hardest and the most important. The parents who raise genuinely life-ready kids aren't the ones who did the most. They're the ones who knew when to do less, when to trust more, and when to let the struggle be the lesson. That restraint, practiced consistently across four years, is what produces a teenager who arrives at college knowing they can handle what comes next. Not because someone told them they could. Because they've already proven it to themselves.

The outcome every parent in this audience actually wants isn't complicated. A self-sufficient, confident adult who doesn't need to be rescued. Someone who can handle challenges, make smart decisions, and build a life they're proud of. Someone who finds work that's meaningful and financially stable. Someone who doesn't struggle the way you did, or who has the tools to handle struggle when it comes. Someone who is genuinely okay in this world.

That person is built in high school. Not in college. Not at the first job. In the four years you still have your child at home, in the daily conversations and small decisions and moments of difficulty that most parents treat as interruptions instead of the actual work.

The path is clear now. The work is simply walking it, one conversation and one decision at a time.

Your Step-by-Step Roadmap — From 9th Grade to Launch Day

Everything in this book points to one practical question: what do I actually do, and when? This final section answers that question directly. It's a grade-by-grade summary of the most important moves from each chapter, pulled together in one place so you can come back to it whenever you need a clear picture of where you are and what comes next.

Keep this. Use it. Share it with your partner if you have one. Read it again at the start of each school year. It's not a rigid checklist. It's a compass.

9th Grade: Build the Foundation

The goal of freshman year is habits. Not a perfect GPA. Not an impressive activity list. Habits that will carry your child through the next four years and beyond. This is the year to set the tone, and the tone you set now is the one everything else gets built on.

Log into your school's parent portal and check your child's grades in every class within the first month of school. Not to react, but to get an accurate picture early. If anything is below a B, address it now, not at the end of the semester. Help your child set up a weekly planning session every Sunday evening, 15 minutes, where they look at the week ahead and identify specific time blocks for studying. Do this together for the first month, then hand it over to them completely.

Have the first low-pressure college conversation in the car, not at the dinner table. Start with curiosity about your child as a person, not with college as the topic. Ask what they've been enjoying, what's been interesting, what they'd do with their time if school didn't exist. Listen more than you talk. Open the channel before you need it for harder conversations.

For extracurriculars, focus entirely on exploration. Let your child try things and quit things without making either feel like a big deal. Pay attention to what they keep coming back to on their own. That pattern is information. Don't sign them up for activities because they look good. Sign them up for things they're actually curious about. Start with in low-commitment opportunities first.

Coach your child to handle one difficult situation with a teacher or coach themselves, with your preparation beforehand but without you intervening. Let them make the ask, send the email, have the conversation. Whatever the outcome, the experience of doing it themselves is worth more than the result.

10th Grade: Find the Thread and Go Deeper

Sophomore year is where exploration starts to narrow into direction. The goal isn't a finished plan. It's a thread, a pattern of genuine interest that connects what your child enjoys, what they're good at, and what they might want to pursue more seriously.

Do the thread-finding exercise from Chapter 3 with your child this year. Set aside 30 minutes, ask the four questions, write down the answers without commenting, and then ask which one they'd want to explore more. Help them find one concrete opportunity to go deeper into that thing before the school year ends. Not a prestigious program. Just the next level of real engagement with something they already care about.

Before course selection, schedule a meeting with your child's school counselor. Bring the current transcript. Ask directly which courses are the right level of challenge for next year based on what the counselor has seen. Then make the final course decision together with your child, based on both interest and readiness. Rigor matters, but only when your child is genuinely prepared for it. A strong grade in a well-matched course beats a mediocre grade in an overloaded schedule every time.

When the PSAT score report arrives, pull out the subscores and find the two weakest areas. Set up a free Khan Academy account linked to your child's College Board account. Have your child spend 20 to 30 minutes, two or three times a week, working specifically on those skill areas. Put it on the calendar like any other commitment.

Start the weekly reflection habit this year and keep it going. Every Sunday, one casual question: "What was something hard this week, and how did you handle it?" Keep it brief. Keep it conversational. The habit of noticing their own experiences and reflecting on what those experiences taught them is the foundation for every college essay and every job interview your child will ever face.

If your child has any opportunity for a part-time job or meaningful family responsibility, treat it as skill-building, not just obligation. Ask them what they're learning from it. Help them connect the experience to who they're becoming. Those conversations turn ordinary life into real preparation.

11th Grade: Execute with Intention

Junior year is the most important academic year in the application. It's also the most emotionally demanding year for most teenagers and most parents. The families who get through it well are the ones who had a clear plan and protected their relationship with their teenager at the same time.

In the fall, register for the SAT or ACT based on which practice test produced the stronger result relative to your target school ranges. Build a prep schedule of 30 to 45 minutes, four to five days a week, focused on the specific skill areas that showed up weakest on the practice test. Take the first real test in October or November. After the score comes back, identify the two or three areas where your child lost the most points and focus all prep on those areas before the second attempt in late winter or early spring.

Build teacher relationships this semester, not in spring. Help your child identify two teachers who genuinely know them and whose class connects to their interests. Coach your child to show up to help sessions, contribute to class discussions in real ways, and share things that connect their classwork to their actual life. In April or May, help your child ask for recommendation letters in person, with enough advance notice to give teachers the entire summer. After the ask, help your child prepare a one-page brag sheet for each teacher including specific moments, what they learned from them, what they're proud of, and what they hope to do after high school.

Start the college essay brainstorming process in the fall using the three prompts from Chapter 4. Don't pressure your child to have finished answers. Have them write one paragraph about one specific moment from the last year, save it, and do it again once a month for the rest of the year. By summer, they'll have a bank of real material to draw from instead of a blank page and a deadline.

By the end of May, have a working college list of ten to fifteen schools, each labeled as reach, match, or safety. For each school, look up the current acceptance rate, the middle 50% GPA and test score range, and the net price calculator result for your family's income level. This research takes a few hours and changes every decision that comes after it.

Protect the relationship this year. Create one regular moment each week that has nothing to do with school or college. Ask your child what they need from you and take the answer seriously. Watch your own anxiety and find somewhere other than your teenager to put it. The parent who stays calm and connected during junior year is the parent whose child comes to them when something goes wrong. That access is worth more than any amount of grade monitoring.

12th Grade: Execute, Submit, and Let Go

Senior year is about executing a plan that's already been built. The foundation is laid. The story is developed. The job now is to get the application out the door cleanly, handle whatever comes back with grace, and begin the final and most important handover of your child's life back to them.

Build the deadline calendar on day one of senior year. Every school, every deadline, every financial aid form due date. Work backward from each deadline and mark the date by which every piece of that application needs to be complete, two weeks before the actual deadline for Early Decision and Early Action schools, and no later than December 15th for Regular Decision schools. Pay attention to the deadlines for your in-state universities — remember they can be as early as October 15th. The families who miss deadlines or submit rushed applications are almost always the ones who treated the deadline as the starting line.

Do a full application review together before any submission. Read the entire application as a package and ask one question: does this tell a coherent story about one specific person? Check every activity description to make sure it answers both what your child did and what it produced. Read every essay out loud. Check every school-specific essay for the correct school name. Make sure nothing you read was written by you.

File the FAFSA as close to October 1st as possible. Look up your state's priority deadline and treat it as the real deadline. Gather everything you need before you sit down to file: Social Security numbers, prior-year tax return, bank account information, FSA IDs for both you and your child. Run the net price calculator for every school on the list before applications go out so the financial picture is already clear when award letters arrive.

Before decisions come in, have the honest expectations conversation. Selective schools reject most of their applicants. Being rejected from a school with a 12% acceptance rate doesn't mean your child wasn't good enough. Make sure your child understands this before the letters arrive, not after. Ask them which schools on their list they'd genuinely be happy attending. Make sure there are real answers to that question.

When a rejection comes, give your child one full day to feel it without trying to fix it. Then, when they're ready, ask the forward-looking question. If your child wants to pursue a waitlist, help them write a letter of continued interest using the three-part structure from Chapter 5. Regardless of wait-list status, make sure they accept an offer and pay an enrollment deposit at a school they're genuinely happy about by May 1st.

And then, sometime in the spring, after the dust has settled and the choice has been made, take a moment together. Not to review the outcome. To reflect on the process. Ask your child one question: what's something you're proud of from high school that has nothing to do with where you got in?

Whatever they say, that's the answer that matters. That's the thing they built. That's the person they became. The school they're attending is where that person will spend the next four years. But who they are when they walk through the door is what determines everything that comes after.

The goal was never a perfect application. It was always a kid who knows who they are, what they're capable of, and how to keep going when life gets hard. That kid exists. You helped build them. And they're ready.

Resources

I wanted to close this book with a few additional resources that many families never learn about simply because nobody tells them these programs exist. Some were mentioned throughout the book, while others are resources I've found genuinely valuable over the years.

One of the most important is regional tuition reciprocity programs, which allow students in participating states to attend certain out-of-state public colleges and universities at significantly reduced tuition rates.

Each program has its own eligibility requirements, participating schools, and approved majors, and those details can change from year to year. Always verify current information directly through the program websites.

The information below is current as of May 2026 and is subject to change.

Western Undergraduate Exchange (WUE)
https://www.wiche.edu/tuition-savings/wue/
Participating states and territories include:
- Alaska
- Arizona
- California
- Colorado
- Hawai'i
- Idaho
- Montana
- Nevada
- New Mexico
- North Dakota
- Oregon

- South Dakota
- Utah
- Washington
- Wyoming
- The Commonwealth of the Northern Mariana Islands
- Guam
- Republic of the Marshall Islands
- Federated States of Micronesia
- Republic of Palau
- American Samoa

Midwest Student Exchange Program

https://msep.mhec.org

Participating states include: Indiana, Kansas, Minnesota, Missouri, Nebraska, North Dakota, Ohio, and Wisconsin.

The Academic Common Market (Southern Regional Education Board)

https://www.sreb.org/AcademicCommonMarket

Participating states include: Arkansas, Alabama, Delaware, Florida, Georgia, Kentucky, Louisiana, Maryland, Mississippi, Oklahoma, South Carolina, Tennessee, Texas, Virginia, and West Virginia.

Tuition Break Program (New England Board of Higher Education)

https://nebhe.org/tuitionbreak/

Participating states include: Connecticut, Maine, Massachusetts, New Hampshire, Rhode Island, and Vermont.

Federal Student Aid Website

https://studentaid.gov/

Official federal resource for FAFSA information, federal student loans, repayment plans, grant programs, and financial aid updates.

Common Data Set (CDS)

Most colleges publish a document called the Common Data Set, which includes admissions statistics, test score ranges, merit aid information, and other useful data. Search for the college name plus "Common Data Set" to locate it.

College Scorecard

https://collegescorecard.ed.gov/

The U.S. Department of Education's College Scorecard allows families to compare colleges based on graduation rates, average debt, average earnings after graduation, and other important outcomes.

College Navigator

https://nces.ed.gov/collegenavigator/

Federal college search database with detailed information about majors, admissions, graduation rates, campus size, and costs.

BigFuture by College Board

https://collegescorecard.ed.gov/

College search, career exploration, scholarship information, and planning tools designed to help students explore college options and careers.

Khan Academy SAT Prep

https://bigfuture.collegeboard.org/

Free SAT preparation resources, practice tests, and skill-building tools aligned with the digital SAT.

NACAC College Advice for Students

https://www.nacacnet.org/student/

The National Association for College Admissions Counseling (NACAC) provides resources and education for students, parents and admissions and counseling professionals

QuestBridge
https://www.questbridge.org/
QuestBridge supports high-achieving, low-income students with opportunities and scholarships for both juniors and seniors.

The college process can feel overwhelming, especially when families are trying to navigate systems they were never taught to understand. My hope is that these resources help make the path feel a little clearer.

www.ingramcontent.com/pod-product-compliance
Lightning Source LLC
Chambersburg PA
CBHW020342180726
47991CB00021B/2238